WHERE'S THE MOON?

THE SEVENTH GENERATION
Survival, Sustainability, Sustenance in a New Nature
M. Jimmie Killingsworth, General Editor

A WARDLAW BOOK

TEXAS A&M UNIVERSITY PRESS • COLLEGE STATION, TEXAS

WHERE'S THE MOON?

A Memoir of the Space Coast and the Florida Dream

ANN McCUTCHAN

Foreword by M. Jimmie Killingsworth

LIBRARY OF CONGRESS
CATALOGING-IN-PUBLICATION DATA

Names: McCutchan, Ann, author.

Title: Where's the moon? a memoir of the Space Coast and the Florida dream
/ Ann McCutchan; foreword by M. Jimmie Killingsworth.

Other titles: Seventh generation (Series). | Wardlaw book.

Description: First edition. | College Station: Texas A&M University Press,
2016. | Series: The seventh generation: survival, sustainability,
sustenance in a new nature | Series: A Wardlaw Book | Includes index.

Identifiers: LCCN 2016009103 (print) | LCCN 2016011044 (ebook) | ISBN
9781623494506 (pbk.: alk. paper) | ISBN 9781623494513 (ebook)

Subjects: LCSH: McCutchan, Ann—Childhood and youth. | Women music
critics—United States—Biography. | Music critics—United
States—Biography. | McCutchan, Ann—Travel—Florida. |
Florida—Description and travel. | Florida—Social life and customs.

Classification: LCC ML423.M4323 A3 2016 (print) | LCC ML423.M4323
(ebook) |
DDC 780.92—dc23

LC record available at http://lccn.loc.gov/2016009103

Contents

Foreword

Ann McCutchan's *Where's the Moon?* is a memoir centered in the 1960s, a coming-of-age narrative set in the heyday of Florida's Space Coast. The author's parents moved to Florida to follow a more general version of the Florida Dream, the Northerner's sense that something special was happening in the Sunshine State that couldn't be found in the industrial Midwest or old New England. The dream intensified when NASA took over Cape Canaveral and came to dominate the surrounding countryside and small towns. The McCutchan family moved from Ft. Lauderdale to Titusville just as the Apollo program and its predecessors captured the imagination of Cold War America, a time that overlapped with the Kennedy years and the Civil Rights movement, the women's movement, the Atomic Age, the Vietnam War, and the assassinations that shook the nation. This unsettled period of American history coincided with the unsettled adolescence of the young girl—Ann—with her dream of becoming a world-class musician and escaping the small town where the hordes of newcomers lived alongside the more Southern representatives of the Old Florida digging in their heels against displacement by Space Program immigrants from other regions and those who hoped to gain by the growth of the region, including Ann's entrepreneurial father.

It is a riveting story, well told by a seasoned nonfiction writer with an insistently unsentimental view of the world, a cosmopolitan style and sensibility, whose development as a human being and whose outlook on the world, despite a persistent irony, fed on the pride of accomplishment and sense of grandeur that

marked American life in the postwar years. McCutchan's lively
memory is enhanced by considerable research, including interviews with old classmates and folks from the Titusville community, then and now. The story comes alive with a flood of details
that include not only the history of Florida's remaking but also
such passing features of daily life as diet pills, pimple ointment,
hair treatment, concrete block construction, cars, road pav-
ing, fashion trends, food, television and radio, pop music, formal music study (and the trials of finding a good teacher for a
young woman seeking to break the gender barrier among wood-
wind artists, jazz musicians, and professional music in general),
high school life, and above all, for the sake of the series to which
this book makes such a valuable addition—Seventh Generation:
Sustainability, Sustenance, and Survival in the New Nature—
the birds, the mammals, the exotic flora, the beaches, marshes,
and swamps that once formed the oldest Florida and were being
transformed daily by development of a kind that overshadowed
the plume hunting, fishing industry, tourism, cattle ranching,
and agriculture of several generations prior.

Do these matters of cultural and natural history provide context for the life story of the girl and the woman she became, or
does the personal history add a more deeply human touch to the
history of American progress, race relations, gender struggles,
and ecology? McCutchan's deft interweaving of personal and
public history makes such questions irrelevant, or alternatively,
gives a resounding yes on both sides. The interplay of the personal and the public shows us that, in building the Space Coast
on the no-longer wild land that nevertheless still teemed with
wildlife and landscapes that fired the imagination, the perpetra-
tors of the Florida dream and their sometimes unwitting accom-
plices (like the young Ann, whose inner life is revealed so win-

ningly here, or her mother with her history of outdoor life and Girl Scouting) were building nothing less than a world. In chapter 3 ("Where's the Moon?"), with the climactic scene of the moon launch, which took place as Ann's life in Titusville was reaching its ambivalent culmination, we learn that this world began to decline and to all but disappear at the very moment of its greatest triumph. It is a book centered on what a place comes to mean to a person, even a place that the person longs to leave behind, how character and culture interact with a place to create a world, and how the world (or, if you prefer, the *way of life*) that sustains people for a while according to their needs and their dreams may ultimately itself prove unsustainable.

McCutchan's reflections are subtle and never preachy. The narrative does the work; the images carry the day; the reader is left with much to ponder about one's own place in whatever world represents the enactment of the current dream, or whatever world seems to be emerging on the horizon where nature meets culture. The book stimulates exactly the kind of reflection and storytelling to which this series is devoted.

M. Jimmie Killingsworth

General Editor

WHERE'S THE MOON?

Prologue

The last time I saw my mother alive, in her fullness, we were standing in the graduate dorm parking lot, North Campus of the University of Michigan, hugging good-bye. It was early September 1974. "Let me know what happens next," she said cheerfully, anticipating, as she most always did, good fortune. "I think you're all set."

Really? I thought. How could she be so sure? We both knew I was here out of an almost unwieldy desire, and an enormous, erratic impatience with the place I'd left behind: Titusville, Florida, a Southern town of forty thousand outside the Kennedy Space Center. Yet I had only been able to reach Ann Arbor on the wings of her steady confidence in me, and now that I'd made it, it was high time for her to drive back to stupid Florida, as I'd been calling the Sunshine State for years. Time for her to leave me to my future in the progressive North, to claim the person I hoped to become.

Already, I'd griped to myself, she'd overstayed her time helping me move into the dorm, gliding about campus in a pleasant trance, as if reliving her own college years at the University of Maine, which she had held out to me, since my childhood, as a golden age. As we shopped Briarwood Mall together for bedding, school supplies, and groceries, I watched her lined face grow increasingly beatific, the wrinkles miraculously smoothing until, it seemed, she was that tall, stately coed from Bangor: Helen Bond, Class of '39, Alpha Omicron Pi, Women's Sports Editor, All-Maine Woman, poised to begin a social service career. Those who knew her remarked on her easy carriage, her empathy, her equanimity.

I hadn't been such a well-rounded undergraduate at Florida State, but a pale, blinkered music major, daily tracing the same path between practice room and rehearsal hall, a self-directed reader who once cut academic classes two weeks straight to burn through all of Hermann Hesse; I was the sort of student I admit I am partial to now, as a professor. My career goal was wholly unpractical: a specialty in clarinet performance, pure folly then, when men dominated the world of professional clarinet playing. But I didn't care; it was what I felt called to do, and my mother knew it, and encouraged it. Although Michigan's generous scholarship package was not enough, and she and my father—back in Titusville worrying over his failing insurance and mortgage business, his ailing prostate—couldn't afford to make up the difference, she had challenged my despair. "Look," she'd said a few months earlier, sitting me down in my Tallahassee apartment. "I'm driving you up there, installing you in the dorm. I've found $500 for you to open a checking account. After that, you're on your own, but I know what will happen: you're so good *they're* going to find a way to keep *you*."

But as she strolled about the Michigan campus on those crisp midwestern fall days, smiling, youthful, it didn't occur to me she was imagining her eldest daughter's future, not reliving her past. I couldn't, or wouldn't, see a mother's pride; in the process of detaching, it was too much for me to bear. Instead, I willed her to return to backward, artistically barren central Florida and leave me alone.

My mother did leave, in a manner unexpectedly complete. Less than two months after she turned back south, she and my father died in an automobile accident just outside of Titusville, on their way to visit friends on the other side of the state. My younger sister had a year to go at college; our parents, fifty-seven and sixty-eight, had looked forward to the freedom an empty nest offered. Instead, their lives were ended abruptly by a young man driving on the wrong side of the road.

((((((

Tragedy of this scope influences, shapes, or dictates personal responses to follow. One reaction, not unusual, is to avoid the scene of the painful incident, which I did. For many years, it sickened me to think of returning to Titusville, to come even close to the Space Coast region—and anyway, there was nothing there for me, I thought; it was just as devoid of art and culture as when I had come of age there.

But in 2011, the year I turned sixty, three years older than my mother had been when she and my father died, I was beset by a relentless admonition to go back, one as deep and demanding as that which had propelled me to leave so long ago. Now it seemed it was my calling to stand quite still in that town, take in its environs, and remember as fully as possible the years of my family's life there, which almost exactly encompassed the Apollo Space Program; indeed, I graduated high school in June 1969, one month before Neil Armstrong set foot on the moon. Besides historic significance and my family's efforts to adapt to a new community, that period was, for me, fraught with the urgency to find appropriate teachers, mentors, and fellow aspirants—a nearly impossible task in a backwater just claimed by NASA. On my worst days, I imagined the whole town, down to its ancient vegetation—Spanish moss stirring in the creaking oaks, vines twisted about rusted cars, burred, pollen-heavy weeds—conspiring to hold me back. The burning sun pressed on me, the drenching humidity smothered, drained me of energy. In returning so many years later, I would confirm the distance I'd achieved, my liberation from each grasping tendril and pounding ray.

That year, around the anniversary of my parents' deaths, I

happened to have a break in my schedule and left Texas, where I live now, with my dog Cole, and rented a bungalow for a month in Titusville, on the Indian River, straight across from the Space Center, the great installation that attracted my father, a businessman, to the area in the early 1960s, and where my mother worked for a time as secretary to a NASA engineer. Each morning, as the sun rose over Mosquito Lagoon and the great Vehicle Assembly Building, I carried my coffee to the bungalow's thatch-roofed patio, inhaled the stiff salt wind, listened to palm trees' rittle-rattle, watched squealing gulls wheel and glide. "Because this place did not hold me," I wrote the first day, with some arrogance, "and in a sense, ejected me, even as I rejected it, I can claim some measure of detachment, even as decades-old emotions clutch me in a fever, as they will, when one visits the scene of a struggle."

Yet I found in a month of near-silence that much of the old distance closed. It's true, that heartache ties you to the place that generated it. In a short time, I had to admit that a mixed, yet undeniable affection for this shambled town, an unlikely mix of rednecks and rocket scientists, had lain hidden for years, alongside my enduring love for my parents. I even noticed, with surprise, that I still possessed an indwelling familiarity with the quirks of living in Florida. This happened one morning when I loaded Cole into the car for a trip to the beach, and as we rolled out toward US 1, a steady, rhythmic flapping sound started up from the car's underside. I did not give it a thought. On we drove, nearly forty miles, to the dog-friendly sand at New Smyrna, and on the ride back, accompanied still by that flapping, it occurred to me that, were I in Texas, I would have checked the source of that sound hours ago. "OK, OK," I said to the responsible voice that butts in on intuition, "I'll look." I pulled over to a stop and crouched to peek beneath the car. Of course. I'd known it all along, without articulating it, even to myself. It was only the end of a scuttled palm frond, a dry little hand caught in the machinery, a sound I'd metabolized decades ago. Eventually, I knew, the frond would disengage and cartwheel off to the roadside, no harm done.

The experience startled me, though. That sound was as innately familiar as the opening of the Bach cello suite I used to play on my clarinet. It was even, I had to admit, a kind of music, my first love and profession, even my salvation, for so many years. Distance, eh? How could one claim it, when one's very blood engaged so with an errant scrap of foliage? Should I admit the obvious, that despite my travels, I'd dragged Florida along in my psychic undercarriage?

Suddenly I understood that, though our years in Titusville were the culmination of my family's Florida sojourn, and that of a nation's particular goal, they weren't the whole story. We had moved to Florida well before the space program ramped up—to glamorous Fort Lauderdale, from Washington, DC, when I was five, participants in the postwar migration, seeking and expect-

ing prosperity. We had been part of a larger picture, as every family is, and failing to acknowledge it now would be to resist understanding my parents, as well as myself.

That scrap of palm reminded me how a landscape lays claim to people; it is not mere backdrop, but context. It holds meaning. Still, in

attempting to write about my experience of Florida and my family's relationship to the state, I can claim no more than a fondness for inquiry and a slight talent for memory, with its vagaries and speculations. In *The Wisdom of Insecurity*, Alan Watts wrote: "Memory never really captures the essence, the present intensity, the concrete reality of an experience. It is, as it were, the corpse of an experience from which the life has vanished." By extension, the harder a writer tries fixing memories to the page, the deader the memories become. One notices more the fixative, the glue dried around the butterfly, than the winged creature that once sailed gaily in time.

Yet I have questions to pursue, ideas to fritter with, and must go along with Proust's notion that experience embodied in a material object only remains captive until "we should happen on the object, recognize what lies within, and set it free." Which would require of me, I think, freedom of movement, an observant eye, and a delicate hand. All of these things I would need, for during that month in the bungalow I realized I had come, not just to remember my parents, to feel once more my heart tighten and explode with grief, but to catch the pieces as they fell, arrange them as best I could to take on light and loft. The notion came over me, typically, on another drive—this one through the Merritt Island National Wildlife Refuge marsh at dusk, where, on a breast of sand away from the launchpads, I found myself weeping at the sight of a snowy egret, dip-fishing the waters with its slim black bill. Although it was winter, and half the scrub was gray and dilapidated, I knew that here, where tropical and subtropical life converge, what looks dead is only dormant, and I was struck to the heart by a kind of truth, a benediction, and uttered it aloud as the sun softened behind a nicked line of wind-toughened palms: "Oh Florida, you're in me—you were in all of us. Now I have to discover how, and why."

Dream State

I

) The Florida newcomer narrative goes as follows: a
northerner—depending on age, finances, or health—is
lured to the state by a job, a business opportunity, or the
climate. His or her neighbors in Milwaukee or Newark are envious; the sky's the limit in Florida, they hear. Land of opportunity, golden as beach sand—Paradise! "Keep in touch," they say,
as the future Floridians depart. "We'll come down to visit!" The
newcomers reach Jacksonville, Apopka, or Coral Gables and settle in. Some aspects of Florida are extraordinary, as envisioned;
some are less so; others are downright disappointing. It's the way
of dreams fulfilled.

Yet one thing is certain: the state's tropical surroundings will
continue to entice and enchant. If your dream takes a dive, your
fall will be cushioned by the bracing perfume of orange blossoms, the plash and boom of waves on flattened sand, multi-
tudes of white, blue, and pink birds posing, arising, flocking,
atomizing in the endless breeze.

(((

Our family moved from Washington, DC, to south Florida in
1956. A year or so later, Dad drove us west through the Everglades toward Naples to see some land he'd bought off a map.
Ten acres! My younger sister Estalene and I, five and seven,
napped through most of the ride. You couldn't converse in a car
without air-conditioning. The wind whipping through the open
windows, the pavement's gritty roar, were too loud, and you'd

wind up shouting at each other. Instead, we accepted the comfort of not speaking, playing with a toy, dozing off without notice, awakening when the car finally left the highway for a white sand road, apparently leading nowhere. The car slid around on the softness, and we slid around in the back seat, giggling. "Where is our land, Daddy?" we cried. "OUR land?" We were in the midst of undeveloped pine flats, miles of it—heard nothing but the rasp of pine needles, a mockingbird's mimicking calls, the Fairlane's snores. On we rumbled, the car nearly bedding down twice, Mom, patient, finally venturing, "We must be close," or, "Should we be watching for a realtor's sign?"

Eventually, the unchanging landscape yielded a few orange survey markers, and a bevy of black-and-white cows standing around in the sand road, unaware it was a road. Dad honked the horn, and the cows didn't move, so he drove toward them, and they stared at us, implacable, at the last minute clattering into the pines like loitering shoppers told the doors would snap shut in thirty seconds.

"I think our land is right about here," Dad said, eyeing the odometer. "Yes, right about here."

"Do we know for sure?" Mom said.

"Daddy, which one is OUR land?" I cried again. I was excited, now. Big land, with cows! Were the cows ours, too? Could I have a horse?

My father stopped the car, and we all got out, my sister and I tumbling toward the sand in our sunsuits and sandals, imagining adventures among the scrub palmetto, pine warbler nests, armadillo squads. Dad strode to one of the survey markers with the purposeful gait he used when measuring square footage in model homes. He could walk out a room in exact, one-foot lengths. "Ten feet by twelve," he'd say. "I'd be willing to bet the guest rooms are eight by ten." But today, in the pine flats, his measured gait was useless, because nothing was divided, and it wasn't clear what the survey markers marked. "Should be right about here," was all he said, and that was it.

We climbed back into the car for the three-point turn into the scrub, and the slow trundle to the highway. Dad lit a cigarette, holding it in the fingers of his left hand, browned arm slung out the window, as he steered with his right thumb. Mom was mostly silent; though, as a betting man's daughter, I'm willing to bet she offered a positive spin on the outing, something like, "It may be off the beaten track, but it has potential." "And someday it will be ripe for development," Dad might have added. Which is what thousands before him, from the start of the Florida land boom in the 1920s, believed when they also bought land sight unseen in the boondocks of a state made of water and sand, envisioning, then building, hotels, resorts, housing developments. Even Jesus Christ warned against such folly! But it happened, and our family was part of it, the human tide washing, sluicing, eddying all over that flat, shifting peninsula, in search of fortunes, rejuvenated lives, answers to prayers, or simply decent livings.

《 《 《

We moved south because my father, a salesman for the Equitable Life Assurance Society, was promoted to a district managership in Fort Lauderdale. The day he came home from the Washington office to deliver the news, I was dawdling in the back end of the living room in our suburban Maryland Cape Cod, gazing out at my first landscape: a steep sweep of evergreens visible through a wide bay window just washed clean with sweet vinegar and water by John, our handyman. Standing there in the blue-and-white sailor dress I'd worn to the Parkwood School's kindergarten and to the next-door neighbor's to watch the Mickey Mouse

Club show, I had nothing to do but whatever I wanted, and this afternoon I was just watching and listening. It must have been about five thirty when I heard the Hudson sedan pull into the garage, and my father's firm step in the kitchen across the hall, where my mother, a bibbed apron over her day dress, was starting dinner. He was still wearing his businessman's fedora, taupe with a black band, as he strode up to her, arms spread wide, and announced, "Well, we're moving to Florida!" My mother dropped her spatula, leaving the pork chops popping in the skillet, and, smiling wide, cried, "Oh, Mac!" as he, a good four inches shorter than she, but solid and muscular, picked her up by the waist and swung her around and around the dinette table, like a doll.

Their spontaneous joy thrilled me—we would move, we would GO!

Little did I know the two of them, especially he, had moved and gone a number of times already. My father, about to turn fifty, had, I would learn later, spent nearly half his years seeking his place, or, a better place. Now he, like so many Americans riding the postwar boom, had been invited to Florida, the nation's Dream State. It was more than advancement. It was a lucky break.

In memory, I'd attended the Parkwood School in nearby Kensington for months, and this move would disrupt a pleasant routine. I can see the open layout of the large rectangular kindergarten room, organized by activity areas, from which children could choose to play for prescribed periods—once you selected an area you had to stick with it. My favorites were the corner offering large, colored blocks from which a child could construct barricades, castles, or less specific structures, and across from it, the nest of tables equipped with paints, crayons, and lots of blank vanilla paper. Less inviting was a space equipped with kiddie kitchen appliances, table, and chairs, for playing house. By its entrance hung several child-sized aprons; once, a freckled boy donned one and drew giggles from the girls.

I suppose significant occasions grow outsized as time passes, for I didn't attend Parkwood very long at all—a letter from the teacher, a Miss Sarabeth Smith, proves I was on site merely from Tuesday, September 4 to Thursday, September 20: thirteen days. I had anticipated kindergarten so eagerly; perhaps that is why fewer than three weeks at Parkwood stuck with me like an entire year. Or was it the abrupt break, the quick exit that enameled those scenes so surely? Other Washington images arise, in no particular order: walking along the wide Potomac with my parents in spring, among pink and white blossoming Japanese cherry trees; running across the grassy lawn at Mount Vernon, George Washington's manse, in a white pinafore; being pushed in a large gray buggy through the National Gallery of Art— the buggy, perhaps brought down from my mother's childhood home in Maine, was old, and could be configured like a giant stroller, a pram. Besides a small child, my mother could stash her sweater, purse, and Kodak in the seat. In the museum, she often paused to photograph masterpieces she admired.

My mother did not work when my sister and I were small and occasionally took cabs into the city to shop at Garfinckel's or even Woodward and Lothrop, while a uniformed babysitter, a jolly Polish lady we called Nursie, cared for us. Once in awhile I went into the city with Mommy, riding the trolley to a specialty grocer, the brakes' metallic squeal searing the ear; stopping by M. E. Swing's Coffee on E Street, the woodsy, chocolaty fragrance of roasting Arabica beans hanging over the entrance; inside, red painted coffee bins lit up the fragrant mahogany cavern. Here, at Christmas, my mother ordered tea and coffee for her father in Bangor.

Closer to home: forest strolls at Rock Creek Park, the dog-woods blooming bridal white, and the park's arched Boulder Bridge, fairy-tale rustic, beneath which, surely, trolls hid. Along the right side of our house, my mother kept garnet roses. Their syrupy scent carried to the screened porch, where my parents made hand-cranked peach ice cream on warm days. My sister and I licked the paddles. One spring, my mother and I planted a pear sapling at the backyard's center, where it would receive full sun. Together, we firmed the squooshy mud at its base with our bare hands, and from the bay window back of the dining room monitored its growth, its spindly arms lifting, lengthening, ever so slightly that summer. In winter, in my navy-blue snowsuit, I huff-puffed with my father up the back hill, pulling a red sled to a line of spruces up top, settled within his protective embrace, and pushed off, sliding, the two of us laughing, hollering, bumping—booomp!—into the red brick back of the house.

Indoors: the mild kerosene odor of freshly waxed wood floors, the scratch of a forest-green sofa where Daddy read aloud to me as I snuggled into his shoulder. And then, my parents' occasional cocktail parties, from which I was naturally excluded, yet the sounds, the aftermath, linger. I'd be put to bed before everyone arrived but lie awake, excited by the repeated ding-dongs at the front door, the exclaimed greetings, the fancy rustle of women's skirts, tinking martini glasses, the grown-up odor of cigarette smoke, murmured conversation, rising and falling, random outbursts following, I guessed, a hilarious, well-timed tale—my father's? Once, someone asked to meet me, and my father appeared upstairs, scooped me up, and carried me down to the landing, my bare toes just touching the polished banister, as the guests gathered 'round and cooed. The morning after the party, I found pleasure in what was left: a scatter of hemmed linen cocktail napkins in pink, yellow, and chartreuse, glass cigarette trays full, a nut dish of furrowed silver, with a few deliciously oily peanuts lolling in the bottom. These, I plucked out for myself before my parents descended the stairs, clearing their throats, still tying their robes.

I'd been taught, firmly, never to enter their bedroom if the door was closed, but one morning I forgot about the rule and burst into their room to exclaim about something, and saw Daddy and Mommy together in one bed. Their heads, side by side, on one pillow. Her dark hair tumbled, his cheek against hers. "Why is Daddy in Mommy's bed?" I asked. They smiled, laughing gently. "You know you're not supposed to come in," one of them whispered. But they didn't ask me to leave. I took a few steps toward them, drawn by a force I can't adequately describe, but understood it then, and still understand it so, as love.

By any measure, our move to Florida was motivated by that, and by so much that had come before.

《 《 《

Every Florida dream has a backstory; by the time we arrived in the state, my parents' were decades long. He, a midwesterner who never learned to swim, and she, a New Englander in thrall to mountains and a rocky coast, might have remained closer to their respective birthplaces, if not for circumstances that set each on long roads away from home.

My father, born in 1906, grew up on a southern Indiana farm planted mostly in wheat, with a substantial crop garden for the family's use. When I was young, his father, two brothers, and two sisters, all living in Indiana or Missouri, reunited when our family visited, and Dad, the only one who had ventured far afield, fell right in with them at the farm. On a Sunday afternoon everyone, with assorted offspring, made a circle of tulip-back lawn chairs beneath the wide oak in the front yard, and shelled peas, or played with Grandfather McCutchan's dog, Shep—one of a long line of Sheps, stretching back to century's turn. And talked. Remember when little Ed stood too close during hay cutting and got nicked on the hand by George's scythe? Ed's forty now, and he still has the scar! Remember when Great-Aunt Roxie learned to drive on that road next to the hog pens? Them hogs sure got out of the way! Remember when Clara soloed at Bluegrass Methodist and instead of "I love to tell the story, of unseen things above," she sang, "I love to tell the story, of unthings seen above"?

As I played hide-and-seek with cousins in the cornfield, gathered eggs from beneath warm chicken bottoms, and rolled in the fragrant barn hay, I imagined my father's upbringing as a pastoral dream, where one had fun with piglets and ponies all day and gorged on platefuls of fried chicken, corn on the cob, fresh tomatoes, and apple pie at night. When he was young, I thought, life was easier, while mine, at eight or ten or fourteen, was complicated by tests at school, not enough cute clothes, boys I liked who didn't like me. It never occurred to me the others thought our lives in sunny Florida exotic, or that my father had ever wanted to leave cozy McCutchanville.

Yet I sensed a lack of connection between Dad and his father, a tall, blue-eyed Irish farmer in clean overalls, gray, eighty. In photographs of the menfolk, Grandfather McCutchan stands slightly apart from the three stocky, brown-eyed sons who took after their long-dead mother. He hovers at the white margins of snapshots, while his offspring stand firm and solid, shirtsleeves rolled up to reveal muscular forearms, like men in Depression-era murals celebrating the American worker.

Much later, when I was in my fifties, a cousin nineteen years older explained. When our fathers were young, our grandfather was known to pose as a gentleman farmer while his children worked the crops. For some reason, he singled out my father and hers for physical abuse, beating them for minor infractions, like dropping a forkful of hay. Each night, after putting up the tools, feeding the horses, and eating dinner with their older brother Melvin ("He stood apart from the rest") and sisters Estalene ("outgoing, lots of friends, died young"), Clara ("glamorous"), and Lois ("strange, private, ingrown"), George and Lloyd, who shared a room in the farmhouse, dressed each others' wounds, hoping for a reprieve. When it didn't materialize, my father got Lloyd, exactly two years younger, to join him in secret, lifting an iron bar back of the henhouse to build up their muscles. One day, Grandfather went after my father and my father challenged him head-on. My grandfather withdrew and never attacked him again. That night, when a train whistle sounded nearby, George said to Lloyd, "Hear that? I'm going to be on one of those. Soon as I can, I'm getting out of here."

My father's Florida dream might have begun that early. During those years, an Indianapolis entrepreneur named Carl Fisher—dubbed "The Hoosier Barnum"—visited the Miami area, at the time a mosquito-infested hell, and proclaimed it the kingdom of heaven. "Look honey!" he exclaimed to his wife, "I'm going to build a city here! A city like magic, like romantic places you read and dream about, but never see." In 1914, Fisher began politicking governors for a new Dixie Highway spanning Indi-anapolis to Miami; it opened in 1916. Not coincidentally, he'd bought land at the southern terminus and became a major devel-oper of Miami Beach, a primary architect of the 1920s Flor-ida land boom. He and his beachfront mansion were all over the Indiana news.

My father finished high school in 1924, close to the height of that boom and during a slump in Indiana farming. Because Mel-vin had left home to work at the new Dodge-Chrysler plant in

Evansville and Lloyd had followed suit, he stayed on, bringing in the crops, attending the University of Evansville part-time on his own dime, because his father refused to send any of his children to college (the youngest, Lois, would make it all the way to Purdue, funded by a well-heeled Evansville woman who'd watched the bright McCutchan kids miss out, one by one, and finally stepped in, no arguments, please). His transcripts show he enrolled for ambitious loads, then dropped courses midterm or even flunked one. When I asked a long-time school administrator about the pattern, he said, "It happened a lot with farm boys back then. Say, when the soybean crop was ready, they had to stop everything, get back to the fields."

But there was another gap in my father's roughly two-year college record: a semester when he wasn't registered at all. My cousin revealed the reason. "Your dad," she said, "took time off to marry a local girl, a match no one thought would last, and it didn't." I was shocked to realize everyone in the family, except my sister and me, had always known this; we'd been kept from the whole story by our sheltering parents, their deaths, and our physical distance.

In 1925, when he was nineteen, Dad married, and his mother died. Grandfather, who had lost a previous wife to illness, burned all photographs of the second, though two pictures survive: a pre-wedding portrait of a full-cheeked Evansville girl in a tailored dress and feathered hat, and an outdoor scene of a thin, sallow farm wife surrounded by various small children, her sparse hair pulled into a bun. Her prosperous father had given the first twenty acres to start the farm. After her death, my father must have decided his responsibilities in McCutchanville were finished and left his young wife and the township, with or without plans to return. I knew some of how he made out. Aunt

Lois once told me Dad sold nylon stockings door to door, ped-dled Karmelkorn in San Antonio, worked as a carnival roust-about and a pool hall bouncer. I thought he must have been ter-ribly resourceful, to make it through the Depression by his wits and hands.

"But Ann," my cousin continued, her voice dropping to a whisper, to deliver the worst.

What could it be? Had Dad done time? Killed someone?

"Ann," Pat said, "Ann, he *gambled*."

My father? The church usher whose sound judgment kept him on the finance committee year after year? I tried picturing the middle-aged fellow I first knew as Daddy tossing dice into a smoky, crowded dirt ring and shook my head, moving on to the older Dad, an affable man who, in family card games, shuffled and dealt with no hurry, expertly. He was capable of an excel-lent poker face, rather like an inscrutable Indian, olive-skinned, quiet, contained, with the finest screen of pleasantry softening the look, sufficient to the occasion. Unless he was telling a story or laughing, he could be hard to read.

((((((

My mother was born in 1917, the oldest child of a Bangor feed salesman and a nurse. She was a father's daughter, tall and ath-letic, taught from an early age to camp, canoe, and fish. Her tendency and ability to go her own way was a natural gift from my grandfather Bond, an independent man, even for a Maine native. He was the youngest son of a wealthy feed company owner, destined to go into the family business, become a pro-verbial pillar of the community. But a few months into his job, Grandfather quit after his family insisted he join the Ku Klux Klan. Soon after he was initiated, he learned what the KKK did in Maine—harass Irish and Jewish citizens—and withdrew. A copy of the initiation photo, with Grandfather in a white costume, was discovered after he died, and a horrified aunt, a southerner who'd married into the family, burned it.

Removed from the family business, Grandfather went to work as a traveling salesman for a rival feed company, and when it was clear he couldn't afford to live in a "good" neighborhood, his family, horrified he might settle on the poor side of town, helped with a basic, two-story house on Grant Street, some blocks away from the rich. When my mother and her brother, Lyndon, weren't in school, he took one of them on sales trips in his trusty Nash, sometimes weeks at a time. His territory was mostly Down East, toward Machias and the coast; for stopovers and hunting trips, he built a rustic camp—house and outhouse—on a pond near Ellsworth.

Grandfather Bond loved driving the back roads to reach his clients, with whom he would chat easily at length; it's easy to imagine him sitting on a farmer's porch, long legs crossed at the knees, trading stories with his acquaintance, the two men falling into occasional silence with a mutual "Ayuh." He never asked for orders. Instead, he finished the coffee offered by the farmer's wife, the slice of homemade strawberry-rhubarb pie, and said to my mother, "Well, Helen, I expect we ought to be moving along . . ." and my mother would collect the pie plates, carry them to the farmer's wife, and offer to help wash them. A few days later, back in Bangor, Grandfather would call the farmer as if phoning in an afterthought: "Say—suppose you'd want fifty pounds of the same, next time?" And the order was in.

Thus, road trips were not a bother to my mother; she looked forward to them. Although Florida was a long way from Maine, her family knew local snowbirds who drove down the Atlantic Coast for winter holidays, staying in the new motor courts.

Word of citrus bounty and Christmas temperatures in the seventies came back, and the myth of tropical plenty and curious sights like flamingos and alligators prevailed, even through the Florida land bust in 1925–26 and the stock market crash of 1929. Florida meant adventure. Why, even Joshua Chamberlain, Union hero at Gettysburg, president of Bowdoin College, governor of Maine, once bought land near Ocala. Had my mother been invited south, she would have been first in the car.

Her father's sales acumen carried the family through the Great Depression and sent her, an honor student at Bangor High, to the University of Maine in 1935. She majored in the new field of psychology, earning average grades and starting positions on the women's hockey and basketball teams. She joined Alpha Omicron Pi sorority, where she made three lifelong friends named Roberta, Betty, and Louise, nicknamed Squeeze. In 1937, her photo appeared in the Boston *Herald* as UM's representative to a conference on social programs. Like other coeds of the day my mother probably expected to marry soon after graduation; she was pinned to a fraternity boy. But the fellow, son of a man in the hardware business, fell ill, was sent to Arizona to prolong his life or possibly die, and broke off with Helen Bond via delivered flowers and a note.

Whether she needed to free herself of the young man's memory, or realized how free she was in the world, my mother left Maine after graduation in 1939 to work for the Toledo, Ohio, Girl Scouts. The job was a good fit for an outdoorswoman whose father was now visible in Maine as a citizen conservationist. He had led a movement persuading pulp and paper mills to stop dumping waste in the Penobscot River, and protect the Atlantic salmon. She, too, would have an outdoor mission. When she settled in Toledo, she sent her anxious mother a fancy box of face powder, and a note assuring her she was OK. My grandmother

had hoped Helen, the perfect daughter, would marry the fraternity boy and become a leading businessman's wife. Grandmother
Bond was more class-conscious, manners-driven than Grandfather, who'd dismissed his position. Her anxiety may be under-
standable. Her father had died young, and as the eldest of three
daughters, she had gotten a teaching certificate at fifteen to support her mother and sisters and save for nursing school. When
my grandfather met her, she was working in a Portland hospital,
plump and happy. Years later, when a perplexed cousin asked
him how he came to marry our officious, overbearing granny, he
laughed and replied, "Back then, the little fat girl was so much
fun."

In Toledo, my mother found a tailor who'd sew a professional woman's wardrobe for her tall frame—straight, calf-
length skirts and long jackets, a topcoat of glen plaid wool. She
lived with three other working women in a rooming house, and
often missed Maine so much she treated herself to dinner at a
venerable seafood restaurant, the kind displaying fresh, flown-in
catch on crushed ice in the front window. For jewelry, she wore
a bright red lobster pin. When Japan attacked Pearl Harbor on
December 7, 1941, she resigned from the Girl Scouts to serve
the Red Cross, in Indianapolis.

《 《 《

The morning my father left McCutchanville—say, a crisp day in
October, when the last of the corn had been felled and the snow
hadn't come—I imagine he packed a small suitcase and hitched
a buggy ride to Evansville with a neighboring farmer, explaining he intended to hop a train to Saint Louis; Ford, Chevy, and
smaller outfits needed workers. Maybe that's what happened, or
what he might have said to avoid condolences for his mother,
questions about how his father was going to get along alone on

the farm, and when did he plan to send for his new wife?

Vanderburgh County's divorce court records suggest he never sent for her. It appears he ultimately abandoned the young woman, although that can't be the whole story; it never is. In a long-secreted photo of the pair, he, wearing a plain white, open-collared shirt and pressed trousers, gazes out toward the horizon, while she, in a frilly flapper dress of the day, her hair a jumble of curls, clutches his arm and mugs for the camera. ("What was he *thinking*?" my sister cried, when she saw it.) Six years later, in 1931, the court released her from the marriage and allowed her to reclaim her maiden name. My father could not be reached and apparently never showed for a hearing.

Dad never joined the auto industry; it seems he skipped around the country, first by choice, then by necessity, after the stock market crashed. Early on, he spent some time in Wyoming, waiting tables at Yellowstone National Park's lodge and entertaining visitors with dramatic readings. At one point he lived in San Antonio. Here was where he sold Karmelkorn, a treat developed and franchised by a Casper, Wyoming, man. Maybe Dad had met the man at Yellowstone, made a connection.

As a carnival roustabout, he raised tents, assembled rides, pitched concessions—subsistence work in the 1930s, when men signed on with traveling shows for meals and a cot. No one could be sure how long a carnival job would last; discussions ran into the night. Would this one continue to Iowa? Disband in Pennsylvania? Make it down to the Carolinas? That short fellow from New Mexico was fired when a child broke her arm sliding off a horse on the merry-go-round. Maybe word of the accident had spread? Someone said a carnival out of Kansas City needed men, but you'd have to hop a train tonight in Springfield to get in line.

During his stint as a pool hall bouncer, he was again a strongman, confronting troublemakers, breaking up fights. According to family members, he knew exactly when to step in and when to step away.

But in 1940, a year after DuPont introduced nylon stockings at the New York World's Fair, Dad returned to sales, hawking stockings door to door. Somewhere. Fifteen years had passed since he'd left the farm, and he'd never returned. He did call Lloyd occasionally from the road to report on where he was, or had been, or was about to go. My cousin remembered when those calls came; they were momentous. She, her sister and brother, and my aunt, Fern, hushed while her father listened and responded. "Uh-huh, uh-huh, yeah. Yeah? When? Uh-huh. Fern and the kids are fine. Well, watch it, George." But now, Dad had a product millions of women clamored for, and perhaps he could get off the long road for good and focus, at least, on a region.

His stocking days lasted about a year and a half. When the Japanese attacked Pearl Harbor, the day after his thirty-fifth birthday, he attempted to enlist in the armed forces. Every branch turned him down, for flat feet or a TB scar on one lung, depending on who told me the story. He finally signed up with the Red Cross in Indianapolis, to work in rehab recreation.

Here he encountered my mother, who held a recreation job similar to his. For my father, who had watched women for at least fifteen years—how closely, I'll never know—she would be a catch: a no-nonsense woman who didn't apologize for her height, wore little makeup, held an even temper. Although she could flirt, she was no coquette. They met at the end of 1942. By now, the United States was in Europe, and the Axis powers were pounding the Allies. In mid-February 1943, the Germans trounced American infantry in Tunisia—the first American battle with German forces—and the Red Cross ordered my father overseas to help with thousands of casualties. It was time again to gamble. "Marry me now," he said to my mother. "Or we may never see each other again."

This is how some decisions were made then, because who knew what tomorrow would bring? Perhaps my mother took the bigger chance, having had far less road time than her suitor. On the surface, the only thing they had in common was history as high school basketball stars. When Lloyd met her, he drawled, "One thing you can count on, Helen: life with George will never be dull." In February 1943 my parents married at the Indianapolis courthouse, with two Red Cross friends as witnesses. In March, Patton took charge in Tunisia and by mid-May the Axis surrendered. My father's transfer was canceled, an especially welcome bit of news, because my mother was already pregnant.

《 《 《

Helen wanted to have the baby in Maine, and took the train back home. Gertrude Herrick Bond didn't approve of her daughter's husband—he was Irish—and George McCutchan's history as an itinerant salesman didn't please her, either. Altogether, the lineage of the forthcoming grandchild must have annoyed my grandmother, though she carefully supervised my mother's health, probably feeding her the same hearty fare she served when we visited: roast beef, baked Maine potatoes, dandelion greens dug out of the backyard and drenched in cream, molasses cookies big as saucers.

When the baby girl arrived, nine months to the day after the courthouse wedding, Grandmother Bond, heavy-hipped and cursed by a bum leg, galumphed into Recovery, demanding first to know, not the condition of mother and child, but what day, exactly, her daughter had married this peripatetic fel-

low from Indiana. The baby girl was baptized Haverill, uncommon as either first or surname, and with no connection to either family. She had a defective kidney and spent most of her short life in Boston Children's Hospital. Grandmother forever held a grudge against Mom's obstetrician, a Protestant man, as if the birth defect were his fault, and steered friends to Bangor's Jewish doctor, Shapiro. Family members still marvel at the switch, for Grandmother was unfailingly racist.

❨ ❨ ❨

By now, the war was in its final stretch. In 1944, the Western Allies invaded France, and the Soviet Union charged after Germany and its allies. In May 1945, the Germans surrendered, and in August the Japanese followed. Around this time, Helen and George decided to start postwar life in Washington, DC, he as an insurance salesman, she as a secretary at the Pentagon. They moved into an apartment and made friends with another young couple who, enamored of Florida, would one day retire near us. In the late 1940s, my mother became pregnant again and lost the baby. She continued at work. My father's sensible, low-pressure sales approach served him well. He was invited to speak at conferences, and someone nicknamed him "The Communicator."

Now my parents were renting a house in Silver Spring, Maryland, and in 1951 brought a healthy child to term, aided, supposedly, by diethylstilbestrol, a synthetic estrogen mistakenly thought to reduce the risk of miscarriage. Years later, the female offspring of women who took DES, known as "DES daughters," were found to experience various medical problems, including, as I learned myself, infertility. My sister, also a DES baby, was born two years after I was; during her delivery, our mother had an out-of-body experience, aloft like a space being, pondering earth. "I was floating up above, looking down at myself, giving birth," she said.

((((((

As soon as we got to Fort Lauderdale, Mom picked up handbooks for shells, fish, and waterbirds, and within weeks she, my sister, and I had taken to beachcombing, identifying every shell we examined on Fort Lauderdale's generous shore, brushing with our salty fingers the hardened lines of sand from mahogany turkey wings, opalescent pen shells, and the tinkly, coin-like discs nicknamed "Baby's Feet" for the imprint left behind by the squishy animal. In our first cotton bathing suits, clammy, smelling of seaweed, we toted home specimens in a pink tin kiddie sand pail, rinsing them in the kitchen sink, and still, sand gathered in the house, because that's what it does in Florida, adhering to everything: baseboards, windowsills, furniture, and knees, elbows, scalp—like genetic material, you carry it with you.

In the backyard of the old town bungalow we rented the first year, banked by ecstatic flowering shrubs that seemed to have sprung up randomly, leggy or bushy, my sister and I plucked pink hibiscus for hair ornaments and from palms pulled baby coconuts smaller than our fists, removing their brown caps for dolls' teacups. We grew fond of poinsettias that bloomed all year, not just at Christmas, and a wide-spreading poinciana tree with showy red blossoms and springy limbs, from which Dad cut a few green branches to make us bows and arrows for Indian play. For weeks, we couldn't get enough of Apaches versus Comanches on Saint Augustine turf, where sticky brown slugs scooched to slime the concrete patio. Alongside them, lime-green stinkbugs hobbled among the thick blades, heading for good clinging space on the screen door, and Mom discovered one crawler not shown in our Florida insect book, its armature a bright, metallic blue. It was literally on its last legs, so she wrapped it in cotton and mailed it to the Smithsonian's entomology department, which judged it a rare beetle and added it to their collection. We became acquainted with palmetto bugs, the large, impermeable tree roaches that indicate not a filthy house, but a home's proximity to fronds and branches. From massed, plaited leaves bending in light wind, the creepy insects crawled, scuttled, or took flight. In my bedroom one morning, I woke up face-to-face with a two-inch tree roach resting on the wall, its antennae flicking. I screamed and sped to the doorway, as the roach resumed its erratic route to a curtain hem, paused, levitated to the popcorn ceiling, and hung lightly, as if preparing to drop to my sheets. Instead, it zoomed to the white tile windowsill, flattened itself and disappeared between sill and rail.

Indoors, two large box fans thrummed constantly, one in the living room, the other facing the hallway, though the bedrooms received little of that concentered wind. My sister and I, damp from jump rope or jacks on the sunny sidewalk, liked sitting in

front of the living room fan, talking nonsense, just to hear our
voices cloven, ribbed, by the whirring blades. This was before
central air-conditioning became standard in Florida homes.
Everyone expected to sweat out the days, anticipate the kinds of
heat: gentle warm and dewy, burning warm and prickly, blister-
ing and so thick no odor or sound could penetrate it. For relief,
one ducked into a cooled department store or befriended anyone
lucky enough to have a window unit. Our second Christmas, I
received my first bicycle, a turquoise girl's model with training
wheels, and took to racing around the block to cool off, alternat-
ing between being completely "at one" with my bike and watching myself as from the air, a six-year-old girl with a blond Buster
Brown haircut, bent over the handlebars, legs pumping so hard
her training wheels lifted off the ground.

《 《 《

Marjorie Kinnan Rawlings, the Pulitzer Prize–winning author
who celebrated Florida's natural beauty, wrote, "Florida has been
guilty of two major crimes: its forest fires and its delight in cutting down hammocks and orange groves to make sub-divisions."
In the middle of our second year, our family, like so many others, settled in one of those ex-jungles, a community ready-made
on recently parched earth.

Bel-Air was a typical 1950s coastal development, a gridded
subdivision north of Fort Lauderdale across highway A1A from
the ocean, laid out on a series of neatly dug canals connecting
to the Intracoastal Waterway. Some Bel-Air homes backed to
water and had docks; the rest of us could fish from a concrete
perch at the development's edge, a low-water spot frequented
by blowfish, which puffed up twice their size when hooked and
weren't worth cleaning. Technically part of the town of Pom-
pano Beach, the community felt more like an extension of

Lauderdale-by-the-Sea, a village just south of us on A1A, where
Muriel's Exotic Jade House and Supper Theatre lured late-night
revelers with parasol drinks and song stylings by Muriel Turn-
ley, a former vaudeville star in her late sixties, who, we heard,
accompanied herself on a Hammond organ. Muriel, whose dyed
red head emerging from a taxi could be glimpsed from my bedroom window, lived across the street from us and kept a pet
monkey chained to a tree in her backyard. But Lauderdale-by-
the-Sea by day was a peaceful beach town, a pastel community
of family motels with names like Surf 'n' Sand and Miramar,
and a dime store stocked with beach towels and snorkel gear.
Someone was always sweeping bits of shells and sand fleas from
its wooden floors, even as small customers in damp bathing
suits tracked in more, leaving wet flip-flop prints between the
front door and the candy rack. Lauderdale-by-the-Sea offered
the closest public beach to us, as the section across from Bel-Air
was already blocked by condominiums, though I seem to recall
access pathways between buildings and my resistance to them.
Even if the paths were public (and I don't know if they were),
you felt like a sneak and a low-life, trudging through with towel
and beach umbrella, watched, perhaps, by a privileged soul with
a tenth-floor view.

Our home on SE Sixteenth Court was like all the others: a
three-bedroom, two-bath cinderblock ranch fronted by wide
picture windows and gay flowering hibiscus bushes. There were
no basements, the water table being so low, and beneath the flat
roofs, no attics to speak of. When we moved in, Dad borrowed a
ladder to inspect the crawlspace up top, and discovered the previous family's Christmas decorations: a frilly silver foil tree and
two boxes of lurid magenta ball ornaments. Such novelty invited
trial; we gathered around the silver spruce that first year and
tossed it to the curb in January.

The front door to homes like ours opened to a living room, with a kitchen off to one side, and to the other, a dark little hall and a warren of tiny bedrooms. At the back of the living room was the Florida room, the state's version of the den or family room. Instead of dark wood paneling, there were jalousie windows and screens, and, in our version, a long, built-in brick planter for snake plants and philodendron, a link to the outdoors, where we spent much of our free time: Dad in a white t-shirt, mowing the Saint Augustine, Mom in her Girl Scout shorts hanging wash on the clothesline, my sister and I climbing and swinging from the ficus tree, playing croquet, or yanking a football-sized fruit from the coconut palm, driving nails into the husk until we could rip it away with our hands and puncture the hairy brown nut. After we drained and drank the watery milk, we hammered the hollow ball until it split open, falling into two or three pieces, and with a kitchen knife, dug chunks of the moist, white flesh, bland as almonds.

In the Florida room stood our first television, our staple programs the *Ed Sullivan Show*, the six o'clock news, and storm forecasts. When Hurricane Donna slammed into Florida in 1960, decimating the Keys, flooding Miami, and wiping out thousands of birds in the Everglades, we holed up behind our boarded windows, riveted to updates until the electricity went out. My sister and I were terribly excited; it was the most violent weather we'd known, a fairy-tale siege. To strike a match in the dark, light a candle, and watch it flare, mesmerized us, a pair of cave girls, huddled in blankets. We ate Dinty Moore beef stew that night, cold, from the can, followed the candle's show of light and shadow playing on the living room walls, as outside, Donna wrapped our home in a furious net of wind and water, slapping the roof and the boarded windows, beating her way through the neighborhood.

Aside from the weather report and news, Dad was not a fan of TV—a waste of time, he called it, though he enjoyed Perry Mason's legal mysteries once in a while. Mom wasn't much interested either, except for *To Tell the Truth*, a show in which three people—two of them imposters—posed as someone with an offbeat job or past, and a panel of celebrities had to guess which of the three was "real." I didn't care, either, though if I stayed home from school sick, I took gruesome pleasure in *Queen for a Day*, where three women testified to unfortunate lives, and the audience, via an applause-o-meter, decided whose sob story most deserved a new washer and dryer. The winner, cloaked and crowned, was led in tears toward her new appliances as Edward Elgar's *Pomp and Circumstance* poured from the studio orchestra.

The TV lasted six years, through our move to Titusville, where, to Dad's satisfaction, it gave out. "Good riddance," he said. A year later, he unwittingly won another as a door prize at a community event, restoring Ed Sullivan to us just as the Beatles made their appearance. But mostly it remained off, a blank, gray glass face reflecting a bit of light, useful as an emergency mirror.

II

In Fort Lauderdale, my father presided over a corner office on Los Olas Boulevard; next to his imposing desk stood a credenza with a formal, hand-tinted photograph of his wife and daughters that made us look like Rockefellers. Occasionally we enjoyed a whiff of real executive glamour, attending Equitable conferences in Key West and New York. We celebrated my eighth birthday in the Plaza Hotel, reveling in luxury: brocade bedspreads, gold bathroom fixtures, formal room service. Daily, my mother, sister, and I struck out for must-sees like the Statue of Liberty, climbing the inside stairs just short of the crown because it was so hot, riding the Empire State Building's elevator to the top, and tramping about Broadway and Times Square, where Estalene and I were taken to our first live musical: *The Music Man*, with Robert Preston. Here, I nearly collapsed of excitement. The tunes, fulsome or lively, rising from the orchestra pit, the actors' voices catching hold of a glittering rope of melody, sending it soaring, looping about our heads, the bright, perfectly cut and detailed costumes, the clever staging—the sum of it struck me hard. At intermission, we scuffed through the powdered, perfumed crowd to the refreshment bar for vanilla ice cream bonbons, coated with a chocolate skin that, with the delicate click of a tooth, gave way to cold, sweet lava. But back in my seat for Act 2, that pleasure subsided as the curtain parted and the orchestra's furious lead-in pulled me into the show like an inevitable lover.

Dad's pleasures were simpler. A devoted weekend golfer, he often spent part of a Sunday afternoon at the local driving range, as Estalene and I, dressed in matching lavender and white seersucker frocks, applauded him, observing that private focus trained on stance, a stick, and a ball he whacked way over the nets. It was quite an intimate view of him; here, we were given access to something unarticulated, golf being an internal game, not a team sport. He let me in on one of his secrets later, when he taught me to play tennis, which he and Mom had enjoyed together at a Washington, DC, country club. Each time I waved my racket at empty air, he said, "You're too close to the net. Stand back, watch carefully, and move to *meet* the ball."

He joined the Kiwanis Club, and Estalene and I played with his fellow members' children at beach picnics and pancake breakfasts as he regaled the adults with stories, most of them poking gentle fun at human foibles, like forgetfulness, laziness, or follies gone awry. I might not recall the tales, but I can hear clearly the vocal gestures in his confident baritone, drawing listeners with easy authority like a seasoned, Twain-like storyteller. He never raised his voice; it was all in the timbre, tone, and phrasing—and following that, dialogue in which he carefully differentiated characters' voices by pitch and density. This, from a man who, when singing hymns at the First Methodist Church, seemed to be tone deaf; in a pew, he droned like a lathe or saw.

Sometime during the Fort Lauderdale years, he made the newspaper when he joined a real estate company. There was his professional headshot, like any other serious businessman with a receding hairline, wearing the dark-rimmed glasses of the day. I wondered: was he employed by two companies, now? Maybe this was connected to that extra work he did, selling homes in the new subdivisions breaking out west of the beaches. "Sitting on houses," he called it, overseeing model three-bedrooms in places

with names like Margate and Whispering Pines and Plantation.
Many Sundays after church, we dropped Dad at a model home
and picked him up at the end of the afternoon. My sister and
I were always invited inside to sniff the freshly painted rooms,
touch the soft matching furniture, select a cellophane-wrapped
peppermint from the glass dish on the reception table. We gazed
at floor plans spread on the sales rep's desk; a line break indicated a doorway, a circle, a toilet. If a customer—usually a couple, quite young or retired—came in, we stepped aside politely
and wandered into another room, professional browsers pretending we, too, were considering a new home.

(((

My mother, the outdoorswoman, landed her dream job as director of camps for the Broward County Girl Scouts. Occasionally, my sister and I attended her staff meetings in the Fort Lauderdale headquarters, a long, dark cottage surrounded by purple
bougainvillea, its interior divided into quiet offices and gathering spaces. Sitting on the floor with our library books in what
was once a dining room, we observed as Mom ran a meeting
from the far end of a conference table, delivering and accepting reports, inviting discussion, friendly, yet official in her adult
Girl Scout uniform—the grass-green A-line skirt and matching
fitted jacket, the emerald beret and its yellow trefoil. The other
women, we could tell, respected her equipoise, and doted on us
a little.

One woman, Ferrol, who held a similarly responsible position, was our mother's best friend. Occasionally, Mom took us
to visit at Ferrol's house, its generous backyard filled with orange
daylilies and pink double hibiscus, and we played there while
the two women sat in the kitchen or the screened back porch
and talked. I loved those visits—the distant, comforting mur-

mur of two women exchanging ideas, confidences, over coffee, the limpid circlings of butterflies and lily heads in the long grass. Inside, we had to be quiet, because Ferrol's husband, wasted by illness, was often asleep in the spare bedroom, encased in an iron lung. Once I accidentally opened that door and saw the giant silver contraption, like something from outer space, with Ernest's head poking out one end. "Hi," he said, coughing, and I, though trained to be scrupulously polite, failed to disguise my horror. "Oh—hi," I said, "I'm sorry," and backed into the hall, drawing the door softly into its frame.

On weekends, when Mom had to check an active campsite or inspect a piece of swampland property the Scouts were considering for a new retreat, my sister and I usually joined her. I can see the sugarcane field for sale near Lake Okeechobee, and the man, probably the owner, who cut us each a piece of sweet cane to chew. Later, we visited a day camp scooped out of the hammock, and as we drove up, the troop leader called to her charges, "Mrs. McCutchan is here!" inspiring a madness of neatening at the picnic tables.

Physical discomfort never fazed my mother. Once, she returned from an Everglades camping trip with poison ivy: the flesh of her right arm was raw, chewed, weepy, as if she'd been attacked by an alligator, not a plant. I lost my appetite sitting next to that arm at dinner and asked if she might cover it. "It heals better in the open air," she said, matter-of-factly, passing me the peas. In time, she became something of a local celebrity when the Fort Lauderdale *Sun-Sentinel* ran a profile headlined, "No Hatchets and Knives for Modern Girl Scouts." In the article, she bemoaned the increasingly timid, indoor approaches to scouting, and spoke wistfully of "roughing it" in Maine. The accompanying headshot shows her in uniform, her graying hair flying from the beret. Her gaze seems trained on a horizon worlds away from the page; her lips are pleasant, but firm. The cutline reads, "She Remembers Rugged Days."

⟨ ⟨ ⟨

Shortly after we moved south, my mother, knowing I missed my kindergarten in Bethesda, and wanting to ensure an easy transition for me, arranged a tour of several schools, which she invited me to choose from. After visiting just two, I insisted on the least likely candidate for an upwardly mobile family: Calvin Christian Day School—a modest, certainly unaccredited little place housed in the cinder block annex of a homely white clapboard church set on a weedy, chain-linked acre.

I might have selected the progressive school we had just seen, in a modern building that felt like a doctor's office inside, with carefully organized blocks, finger paints lined up chromatically in clear glass jars, and neatly dressed children moving from one circumscribed play area to another. But I liked the cheerful disarray at Calvin Christian, where the kids in homemade cotton hand-me-downs chattered noisily among themselves and the lids on tubs of cheap library paste weren't screwed on tight. Mrs. Winkelman, the elderly teacher, bird thin, slow, and gentle, didn't try to recruit me like the brisk progressive school lady had, on the basis of a long questionnaire my mother had to fill out in a vestibule, before we were allowed entrance to the perfect classroom. At Calvin Christian, the two of us just walked in, sat down on a pair of unoccupied carpet scraps, and joined the group. At once, a dark-haired boy, his white shirttail flying, ran up and kissed me on the cheek, a completely spontaneous act that delighted me in a way no other kiss could, or has, since. What kind of world was this, that a child, a person, could be so taken by another at first sight and embrace them directly without thought?

The dark-haired boy, whose name was Johnny, became my friend for a time; once, my mother and I visited his home, an old Florida bungalow with a dirt yard where he lived with his father, a quiet Italian man whose wife had died or left. Young as I was, I understood why Johnny was so puppyish. Something was missing, he knew it, and he was looking for it.

The rest of that year remains for me a wash of naive group activity centered on crayons, jump rope, and cupcakes: bright and pleasing, but lacking memorable texture. In the June class photo, I stand back row center, a full head taller than the others, having undergone a sudden growth spurt—expressionless, heavy-lidded, dumbstruck. Johnny, who would move at the end of the year, sits cross-legged in front, eyes shining, grinning for the camera.

I enjoyed Calvin Christian so much my parents allowed me to stay on for first grade before the inevitable transfer to a more competitive public elementary school and the climb toward higher education. My mother had already shown me her University of Maine yearbook, signaling the joys ahead, though to me, the book's fixed headshots of Depression-era jocks and coeds exuded the creepy unreality of the stuffed wildlife we'd seen in museum dioramas, no assurance I would be as happy as she had been. Neither did I imagine I would ever, as she had, earn a title like All-Maine Woman, the Pine Tree State's version of Best All-Round Girl. Still, on rainy afternoons, I was drawn to the yearbook's preserved countenances, noting the other students' hometowns and majors, wondering what had happened to them after graduation, and haunted by a bespectacled, buck-toothed girl from Massachusetts named Stacia V. Kufel, as plain and awkward as my mother was handsome and confident. What ever happened to *her*, I wondered. What would happen to me?

Shifting from Calvin Christian's kindergarten to the other

side of the accordion-fold divider, I discovered a one-room school with sturdy wooden desks filled by thirty children, grades one to six; that year, there happened to be no third graders. The teacher, Miss Honnadale, a pretty woman of about twenty-five who wore her chestnut hair in a bun, and dressed in full, calf-length skirts of navy blue or black with white roll-sleeve blouses, began each day with a prayer, and then sat down to the piano, leading all of us in song from a red book containing hymns I hadn't encountered in the rote-taught children's choir of the downtown Methodist church our family attended then. Miss Honnadale always chose the opening hymn, pounding out the introduction so firmly we all vibrated to the proper key before opening our mouths. Often we started with a familiar children's song, like *Jesus Loves Me*, which seemed cloying to me even then, or the military rouser *Battle Hymn of the Republic*, with the bewildering line: "trampling down the vintage where the grapes of wrath are stored." A vintage, I thought, must be an overgrown forest path, leading to a closet of angry fruit.

After that, we children got to choose, and nearly every hand shot up, even those of the sixth-grade boys in the back, who pitched forward at their desks, waving to be recognized over the little heads bobbing in front. The older ones always lobbied vociferously for a gospel hymn called *Peace, Be Still*, a story, really, a dramatic dialogue between Jesus and the disciples, out in a boat on the "storm tossed sea." In the song, the disciples are frightened, requiring a great rumbling in the piano and eliciting a hearty outcry from the boys, especially the fellow whose voice was already starting to change. Then, with an abrupt switch to a tinkly accompaniment, Jesus reassures the disciples—and here, the girls shone like angels—"They all shall sweetly obey my will, peace be still—peace, be still."

Hymn singing at Calvin Christian provided a feast of

language—how many six-year-olds read sentences like "Master, the tempest is raging, the billows are tossing high"?—and introduced me to music notation, which I perceived first as gestural: when the black dots on the staff ascended, the music swept up, and when they descended, the music swooped down. It was spatial, too: a note drawn hollow in the middle could command a whole measure of linear space, all by itself, which pointed to the temporal: a hollow note took more time than a black one—you held it out several beats. Soon I could read stepwise motion— that is, notes in sequence: A, B, C, because the pitches were close together on the staff: space-line-space, and on up the ladder. And then, I could read and sound out triads, or a skip from one note over the next note, to the one after that, like so: A to C, B to D. I didn't know the names of the notes—that would come a few years later—but after I got a melody down, by scanning the score and catching it by ear from kids who already knew it, I sang it passionately by heart, reading the hymn book for the words, which fascinated me.

This was not Mother Goose, Andersen, or Seuss. This was the sound, the vocabulary, of the King James Bible. My mother had taught me the Lord's Prayer and the Twenty-Third Psalm from her copy. In Washington, at bedtime, as I turned on my feather pillow and snuggled into her waist, she read one or the other to me, encouraging me to memorize them. "The Lord is my shepherd" she began, and I repeated: "The Lord is my shepherd." And when I was four or five, she and Dad gave me my own Bible, the cover featuring handsome long-haired Jesus sitting on a rock beneath a blinding blue sky, arms outstretched, speaking to robed children of all ages: toddlers, youngsters, a few taller kids in the back, one holding to a tethered goat or sheep, another grasping a sheaf of wheat. I was discouraged by

the tiny printing inside and didn't attempt reading from this
Bible for years. But I remember the sharp, lavender smell of that
book: the acrid ink, the frail leaves, the stiff buckram binding.
Ancient poets lived inside that smell; they were indigo, pulp,
and fiber. And alongside, the lilt of my mother's voice: pleasant,
firm, a little distant, yet reassuring, because I'd known her measured sonorities from the womb. "Surely, goodness and mercy
will follow me all the days of my life," I chanted after her.

During recess at Calvin Christian, we children played in a
large portion of the weedy lot containing a tetherball pole, a
green wooden sandbox, and space to run and play tag or red
rover. I would build volcanoes and castles in the sandbox if
someone asked me, and enjoyed tetherball, which was active,
required skill, and occasionally involved someone getting bon-
ked on the head and everyone laughing. I also took to walking alone at the perimeter of the playground, which was over-
hung by drowsy coconut palms, long fronds leaning in, rustling,
as if to gossip. My favorite tree was a spectacular traveler's palm,
its trunk a great, scored handle, its greenery a wide, glossy fan,
teasing the sky. Along the fence, scruffy lantana grew wild, its
flower heads of elfin white, orange, and yellow blooms nodding among toothed leaves, which released a cloud of cinnamon
when I crushed them underfoot. And within the fence links,
garlands of honeysuckle arced and twisted, feathered trumpets
quivering in the breeze.

Content along this fence, which seemed not to be a fence,
but an invitation, and inspired by the stories my first-grade
classmates and I whispered in single-grade groups, or by the stories read to all of us, grades together, I began narrating silently
what I observed, telling the tale of the moment, like a voice-
over: "Sam and Tommy ran to the tetherball pole. Sam arrived

first. He grabbed the ball and swung it." Soon, in a move toward
self-consciousness, I narrated my own actions as if I were com-
posing a children's book: "First, Ann walked up to the poinciana
tree. She liked its fuzzy pink flowers. She picked one and sniffed
it. It smelled sweet. Then she walked to the fence and looked out
at the street. She looked up at the sky."

And when I looked up at the sky, past the honeysuckle, the
palms, the poinciana, I began to envision a larger world of my
own making, because it seemed, in the eggy Florida sun, that my
own spirit, entwined with something holy, had been bestowed
on me here, had taken root, and would surely put forth a green
shoot, and another, and another, and one day, flower.

My private stories might take all recess. No one ever singled
me out for unsocial behavior; I could be a whole note, containing my silent beats, alone. And then, just as the desire to read or
sing with the others began to well up in me, Miss Honnadale
appeared in the yard with a brass bell and rang us all back into
the classroom, like a frontier schoolmarm.

When a child experiences the wholeness of silence, the beats
known only to her, she has passed into grace, and despite dis-
tractions, will continue to seek that sublimity, return to it, cultivate it by hook or crook, for it is nothing less than her soul.

III

But by the late 1950s, south Florida's natural landscape had
begun filling with noisy commercial attractions. My sister and
I were taken to the major enticements: Parrot Jungle, Monkey
Jungle, Flamingo Groves, and the Miami Seaquarium, where
we were transfixed by a manatee packed and floating like a load
of wet wash in an open, wishing-well tank. You could touch
its gummy, stinky skin, drawing a reaction from the poor ani-

mal so slight you still couldn't tell which end was which. But
the manatee could talk. All you had to do was push a button at
the side of the tank, and from a small speaker came a woman's
perky voice: "Hi! I'm Sally, the Sea Cow!"

With her Kodak, Mom documented these outings, including an afternoon at a popular African Safari spread, where we
girls posed in our Sunday best, flanked by Dad in Bermuda
shorts and tweed cap, and a tall black man in war paint and a
fright wig. Estalene and I, catching our parents' satirical com-
mentary, and having already discovered *MAD* magazine, developed knowing sneers early on: all of these enterprises were fake,
we knew, even the Jungle Cruise out of Fort Lauderdale to an
"authentic" Seminole Indian village, where friendly natives in
blousy, ruffled patchwork shirts and skirts waved at us from a
riverbank, bidding us purchase coconut husk dolls and gasp

at an alligator wrestling demonstration. We took this trip at least twice—it was a favorite birthday party outing for kids—and the second time, we cynically inspected the rumps of those husk dolls for the sticker appearing on so many of our toys then: Made in Japan. But to our surprise, the dolls were still made by the Seminoles.

We also made a pilgrimage to Vizcaya, originally the winter residence of John Deering, of the Deering McCormick–International Harvester fortune. Built south of Miami on Biscayne Bay along the lines of an eighteenth-century northern Italian villa, the house and its gardens had required a lot of jungle clearing so one could later say the estate was "surrounded" by lush vegetation. That Deering's resources came from farm machinery responsible for a phenomenal increase in midwestern grain harvest must have impressed my father; that Deering was from South Paris, Maine, did not escape my mother. As well, we visited Ca' d'Zan, the Ringling Estate on Sarasota Bay, an outsized elephant of a spread inspired by grand Venetian palaces a fellow with a circus fortune could afford to imitate.

Thus, we came to know two exhibition genres formed in and on Florida's floating muck: safely showcased "wild" exhibits, and lavish, imitation empires. On trips farther up the Atlantic coast, we'd encounter historic landmarks, like those in Saint Augustine, where my sister and I posed at the Old Jail in stocks—in this photo, I'm about to lose my good-girl patience, and she is already well into The Sneer as Mom snaps the picture.

Estalene and I preferred attractions a local guide might wanly recommend as "worth a look." They included lopsided orange juice and souvenir stands, their hand-lettered signs propped up on the highway, some with intentional misspellings to lure out-of-staters amused by native ignorance, some honestly misspelled. Many were small family businesses staffed by

relatives and friends peddling crude alligator handbags, palm frond hats, badly glued seashell sculptures. One of our favorites, on US 1, was Manny's Alligator Farm, featuring a single scabby reptile passed out in a ditch. Manny's might have been the source of a baby alligator Mom sent our Maine cousins one Christmas; the gator occupied their home's only bathtub until it grew to four feet, and the poor thing was supposedly "donated to a wildlife fahm." At another of these stops, Estalene and I spent our allowances on coin banks made of cleaned-out coconut shells and painted with human faces—Jemima brown ones, of course. Mine had pink cheeks and a bandanna around her head, and at her base, a little moniker: "Bonnie, the Nut from Florida." I pitied Bonnie because she was only a head and was lorded over by worse mementoes, like those horrid hanging gorillas flayed out of whole coconuts, hairy husks resembling the coats of primates never seen in Florida.

We repeated some of these trips when Grandmother and Grandfather Bond, recently retired, started migrating from Maine during the winters. By now, Grandmother was no longer wary of her son-in-law; he'd fathered two nice girls and established a conventional career. Just as we represented northern opportunists, they typified middle-class snowbirds. Mom and Dad found them a month-to-month efficiency at the Wee Elf Motel: a mom-and-pop outfit set back from Dixie Highway among pines, its neon elf, peak-capped and pointy-toed, blinking a can-do attitude on and off through the night. They liked the Wee Elf owners, who were probably from Maine. In exile from her home state, Mom had developed a knack for sniffing out Down Easters. Sometimes, she wore the lobster pin on her collar—an identification badge.

Grandmother and Grandfather didn't last long at places like Parrot Jungle, with its streams of tourist kids relentlessly imitating chimpanzees, scratching their armpits and grunting. But, like their counterparts, the elder Bonds enjoyed the warm winters, sitting in webbed lawn chairs under the Wee Elf's pines and watching the passing traffic, exclaiming over so many out-of-state plates. "Saw five from Maine today!" they'd say. I don't believe they had a car in Florida; there were lots of pickups and drop-offs. Grandmother didn't drive—never had, never would. After Grandfather died and her bum knee gave out, she begged rides from anyone going anywhere, just to move through a few blocks of changing landscape. This got on our nerves: "Mommm, why didn't she ever learn to drive?" But no one could fault her desire. Grandfather, ever spry, enjoyed deep-sea fishing for red snapper, on which there must have been no limits, because at least once he returned from a day on the water with a trunk-sized ice chest stuffed with the pink and red fish. He cleaned every one of them at the Wee Elf, and we all came to dinner, crowding around a Formica table meant for two. The meal likely included potatoes, string beans, and a bit of iceberg lettuce, salad being an afterthought.

《 《 《

Once we'd moved to Bel-Air, I decided my weekly allowance wasn't sufficient, and, responding to an ad in the back of a Betty and Veronica comic book, mailed an inquiry about selling tins of White Cloverine Brand Salve door to door. When the information arrived, Dad put his foot down.

"No daughter of mine is selling to the neighbors," he said, leaning back in his burnt orange easy chair, snapping open the *Sun-Sentinel*.

"What about greeting cards?" I asked, proffering a come-on in the back of *Casper the Friendly Ghost*.

"No."

"Why not, Daddy? Why can't I earn extra money if I want to?"

My father couldn't refuse a little entrepreneurship in his daughter, so he said he'd think about it, and came up with two paying jobs my sister and I could do around the house. One was pulling weeds and sandspurs out of the coquina driveway for ten cents an hour, a meditative task I liked, unless I was desperate for money, and then, an hour seemed like a terribly long time for a dime, plus, sitting on broken shells pocked your fanny. The other job was preparing mass solicitation mailings for Equitable. There were five steps that paid:

1. Fold the solicitation letter in three
2. Stuff the letter in an Equitable business envelope
3. Seal the envelope
4. Address the envelope
5. Stamp the envelope

My father brought the materials home in stationery boxes and my sister and I set up shop behind the snake plants in the Florida room. Folding and stuffing each took about the same amount of time; sealing and stamping were accomplished quickly by swiping a wet rag over a staggered row of envelope flaps or a coil of purple Lincoln four-centers, easily pulled apart and applied. Addressing took the longest, for we had to read the tiny print in Dad's reverse-listing telephone book for Broward County and make our little-girl cursive legible, if not business-like. The reverse-list book, organized by address, not name, fascinated and unsettled me. Here was a new way of considering people, even of tracking them. If I wanted to know the names and numbers of everyone on a particular block, all I had to do was look up that street, and there they all were, in a row, by house number. It seemed wrong to me, somehow. When Dad indicated which streets we should address, I understood he was targeting particular neighborhoods.

The content of those letters went something like:

Dear Friend:

As the head of your household, you care for the safety and well-being of your family. You do everything you can to provide for your wife and children, to make sure they have all the necessities of life—and some of the luxuries, too.

To put it simply, your family depends on YOU.

But what if something *happened* to you?

If you were to *die*, how would your loved ones get along?

How would they *survive*?

At the Equitable Life Assurance Society of the United States, we . . .

Everyone knows what comes next.

My sister and I could move a lot of mail when we wanted something badly, like a Betsy McCall doll or a Tonka dump truck. The rate Dad established was one penny for every ten pieces, per procedure. Fully preparing one envelope, then, paid a nickel. Having read about the Industrial Revolution in school, I arranged an assembly line. I might fold and fold, while my sister stuffed and stuffed. The process broke down at the addressing stage, when we toiled at the same task, side by side, my left hand and her right cramping over destinations like Mr. Howard F. Burkenholder, 1416 Poinciana Court, Sea Ranch Lakes, Fla. Yet on we scratched, with our Equitable Life Assurance Society ballpoints, closing in on a trip to Woolworth's.

"A penny every ten," Dad intoned, passing through the Florida room, smiling, approving. "A penny every ten. Good work, girls."

Only now does the quality of his generosity occur to me; for while another father might have hovered over us, coaxing our childish scrawls into professional lettering, Dad seemed not to care that the first impression a prospective client received was that of a ransom note.

To fill the gaps between mailings, Mom offered employment, too, at the ironing board. Pay started at three cents for a sleeveless blouse and ran to six cents for slacks or a long-sleeved shirt.

I had learned to iron under Grandmother Bond's tutelage one summer in Maine, a kitchen lesson that ended in tears because I failed to meet her standard for pressing the fabric around and beneath a button. Over and over, I aimed the thick tip of her heavy, huffing old steamer under a tortoise-shell disk, sliding off center when my gesture was too delicate, popping a thread when too forceful. "No, no!" she'd grunt, pulling the iron out of my hand, shoving me off to the side with her plump hip. "Like this." And she'd execute the procedure so precisely I almost believed it mattered. When I complained to my mother, she admitted a long frustration with Grandmother's perfectionism. "When I was younger, I vowed that when I had children, I would not be like her," she said, echoing legions of daughters, past, present, and since. But she kept her word.

❆ ❆ ❆

On October 4, 1957, a month after we moved to Bel-Air, the Soviet Union launched the first artificial satellite in Earth's orbit. The event failed to register with a six-year-old girl just signed up for tap and ballet lessons, though a few weeks later, she dropped a penny in a gumball machine and received a red plastic ring embossed with a round, spiked symbol and the word "Sputnik."

Sputnik sounded evil, like mischief or wicked or iniquity, from the Bible. Maybe the girl had heard the Miami newscaster her parents liked speak it in a threatening or derisive tone. The following year, 1958, their beloved President Eisenhower—war hero, Democrat-turned-Republican—established the National Aeronautics and Space Administration, NASA—But that didn't register with the girl, either, and neither did any other Cold War rumblings in the years that immediately followed.

Now she was in the fourth grade at McNab Elementary School, over-dosing on biographies of Annie Oakley and Marie Curie, Grimm's fairy tales, and Marjorie Kinnan Rawlings's evocations of Old Florida. Her teacher, an elderly woman who smelled like lavender and chalk and wore faded housedresses and was too retiring, or unwilling, to discipline the naughty boys, managed to calm everyone after lunch by reading *The Yearling*, in a voice as soft and wavy as a distant radio broadcast, while the children lay their heads on their desks. And toward the end of the school day, when the tropical humidity had again silenced everyone, drowsy from the purple solvent pressed into their vocabulary worksheets, the girl tuned in to the strains of the sixth grade beginning band rehearsing in the cafeteria two porticoes over, plowing through scales like a room-sized accordion.

For some time, I'd been in love with music, beginning with hymn singing at Calvin Christian, *The Music Man*, and six years of tap and ballet lessons, de rigueur for little girls, whose mothers took up America's interest in dance after the Russian choreographer George Balanchine cofounded the School of American Ballet and the New York City Ballet. Just as the Cold War was played out in chess matches, it was performed on rosin-flecked stages. In 1961, the year before I was given my first toe shoes and began developing a body that would never hover daintily *en pointe* ("Where did that child get that build?" a studio critic blurted, and glancing at my mother, said, "Oh.") the young Kirov star Rudolf Nureyev's defection dealt a severe blow to the Russians. Yet we pre-pubescent students at the Kathryn Whipple School of Dance, tucked into a sand-whipped shopping center, continued to worship the memory of Russians like Anna Pavlova, who'd been enshrined in a popular children's ballet book. Heads held high, toes pointed until our arches ached, we were, for one hour a week, princesses, ice skaters, swans.

At home, we had a cache of long-play classical records, many belonging to a family friend who left them in our care during a trip to Europe and never retrieved them. Others, Mom had purchased for ninety-nine cents each at the Fort Lauderdale A&P. I remember what she put in the shopping cart to earn that low, low price: Jane Parker apple pie, hard as a hubcap; Spanish Bar Cake, coated with white frosting you could peel straight off like a wig; Ann Page peanut butter, its label stamped with the por-

trait of the ideal housewife—face polished pink, hair neatly
bobbed. But then came the records: Ferde Grofé's *Grand Can-
yon Suite*, Bedřich Smetana's *Die Moldau*, Antonín Dvořák's
New World Symphony. I can see the albums stacked at the end
of the canned meat aisle, luring beach-blind buyers of Hormel
Vienna Sausages with soothing cover photographs of mountains,
rivers, and forests. The albums did not fit into the brown paper
grocery bags, so I was invited each week to carry the new record
to the back seat of the Hudson and gaze at it on the way home.
Once we had pulled into the double garage, I would jump out
of the car, carry my prize past the Styrofoam surfboards in the
utility room, on through the turquoise kitchen and the Florida
room to the living room where the Magnavox stereo—a hunk of
mahogany battened with waffle-weave speaker cloth—stood. I
would draw the new record from its cover and work it onto the
greased spindle so that it dropped straight down onto the turn-
table with a soft plop. Then I would press the "on" button, lift
the tone arm, and poise the stylus over the wide outer groove,
waiting for the gleaming disk to reach maximum speed.

Oh, and once the needle settled into the spinning rings of
perfect vinyl, achieved the delicate friction required to release
the tones submerged in the oily platter, I could attach my own
thoughts and feelings to the violins that soared, the trumpets
that flourished, the bells that pealed. This music—played, no
doubt, by cash-poor orchestras grateful for the grocery chain's
contract—represented everything I wished I could express.
What would I have said, had Mozart and Schubert and Beethoven not spoken for me? Everything from No One Is Sad-
der Than I Am / Will Anybody Ever Love Me / I Am The Center of The Universe—to all of the things that cannot be put into
words but together mean something beyond the inadequate
"God."

《 《 《

On April 12, 1961, Soviet cosmonaut Yuri Gagarin became the first human to enter outer space, orbiting Earth, and less than a week later, the United States, having trained 1,400 Cuban exiles to overthrow Fidel Castro's possibly Soviet-backed government, launched attacks known as the Bay of Pigs Invasion. On May 5, 1961, Project Mercury, America's human spaceflight program, caught up to the Russians, catapulting Alan Shepard into space, drawing every American's eyes upward. The McNab Elementary School talent show that spring was won by two of my classmates, Vincent and Anthony, wearing Reynolds aluminum foil spacesuits and singing, to the tune of a 1902 ditty, The Glow-Worm: "We are moon boys, aren't we funny, we live on ice cream, cake, and honey."

Shepard's feat was a triumph, but the Bay of Pigs effort had failed, and now Cuba seemed, even to fourth graders, like a direct threat. The evil Russians were down there building nuclear weapons for Cuba, and since the closest US target was south Florida, our lives were on the line; we had to be prepared, we had to drill—constantly, it seemed.

Suppose we were parsing a tedious math problem ("Dottie wishes to buy each of four friends a bar of pink soap. Each bar costs five cents. Dottie has twelve cents saved. If she receives a nickel weekly allowance, and plans to save three cents a week toward the soap, how many weeks will it take her to earn enough for the four bars?"), or discussing the differences between subsistence societies (poor) and manufacturing ones (rich, like ours). Or possibly we were decorating a bulletin board with green and yellow construction paper daisies and magazine pictures of pretty women in form-fitting sheaths and aprons for Mother's Day. Or studying for our Florida history test, memorizing as truth that yarn about Juan Ponce de León's quest for a

Fountain of Youth and the gold that was never, not ever, available on Florida soil. In the midst of it all, a siren squealed and we dropped our books and scissors and paste, rushed to kneel backward under our desks, faces pressed hard into the seats, hands gripping the napes of our necks, as if to prevent our heads from snapping off. "Duck and cover! Duck and cover!" the principal, Mr. Keaton, bellowed over the intercom. I thought Mr. Keaton stupid; he pronounced "library" as "lye-berry."

One day we were shown a short film on the looming catastrophe, a frightening piece of propaganda with footage of real mushroom clouds and people running and screaming for their lives. Fidel Castro was pictured in the film, his smug challenge clear in the jutting, untrimmed beard, the black Cuban army beret pushed jauntily back of his forehead, the Havana cigar clenched in his mouth to one side.

On the playground, "Castro" joined "Sputnik" as a nasty word; both girls and boys, playing at anger with one another, could be heard yelling, "I'm gonna send CASTRO after you!" But when ordered to Duck and Cover, most of us got serious— though I always wondered how effective the exercise would be during a real emergency, given the classroom's long wall of louvered, unscreened windows, open most days to the tropical air. Always, one or two children were assigned to race over and crank the windows shut before assuming the classroom foxhole position. Yet, if a nuclear explosion had ever occurred, the glass would have blown into knives and lacerated us all, pinning us to the holiday bulletin board, spearing us to the linoleum floor.

Twenty days after Alan Shepard sailed into the blue yonder, President John F. Kennedy, in a "Special Address to Congress on urgent National Needs" announced a goal of "landing a man on the moon by the end of the decade." On July 21, Gus Grissom rode *Liberty Bell* on a suborbital flight. Six days after that I turned ten, making no note of *Liberty Bell* in my new blue vinyl diary with the pert bobby-soxer on the cover because I was planning a garage revue for the neighborhood, starring all the little girls on our block who took lessons at Whipple's and were willing to bear my directorship—for I was the oldest on the street, by rights the bossiest, and the one who wanted most to perform.

To showcase this entertainment, which parents paid ten cents to attend, my sister and I transformed the garage from a dank concrete cave to an auditorium, never mind the storage cabinets, workbench, and garden tools lurking along the walls. Given two old bed sheets to work with, we devised both a backdrop and a curtain, hand-coloring the cloth with our favorites from a sixty-four-count box of Crayolas—Bittersweet, Umber, Cornflower—and hung them up, the backdrop taped against the cabinets, the curtain strung out between an antique bedstead at one end and an elevated lawn mower at the other. To keep the sheets from lifting in the breeze, we anchored the hems with coconuts harvested from the backyard.

The show is deservedly lost to history, as are the musical choices broadcast on the suitcase record player, though Bizet's *Carmen Suite* and Victor Herbert's *Babes in Toyland* vie for memory's attention, as does Stravinsky's *Firebird* dance, to which I contrived a scene where Maid Marian and Robin Hood escape the Sheriff of Nottingham by hiding behind a red and green plastic inner tube. Our numbers were derived from tap and ballet routines from the previous spring's recital, our costumes unashamedly pulled from the same. Oh, how we skipped and kicked and twirled on the oil-spilt garage floor, lockstep in soft pink tutus, royal madrigal capes, white-and-silver princess skirts, our fluttering feet, our lofty raiment transfiguring us as blithe sylphs, awakened beauties.

White Acres

I

October is south Florida's golden month. Summer's humidity has finally lifted, and the sun, no longer a glaring orb, is a burnished doubloon, hanging over a cooling, swaying ocean. You sense it when, wading out of the water to dry sand, you're caught by a chill, and if you're a young girl, you hurry for the beach towel your mother extends, pass up the blue shallows in which you loitered only last week.

Now, a tepid breeze swoops down Fort Lauderdale's beach; your teeth clatter. You buff the sea floor's sticky grit from your arms and legs, from your checked gingham bathing suit. You lift a cotton shift over your head, feel it settle over your salt skin, catching on a sand blister here and there, and tie the towel around your waist, trudge barefoot through the deep yellow grain closing in over your ankles at every step. Up the slight hill you go, with your mother and sister, to the angle parking under the palms and tall stands of oleander, the fragrance enfolding you, whirling around your damp head like a rope of taffy, and you slow down, you can't help it, the heavy sand, the pull of blooms, your body exhausted by the pounding, sucking Atlantic.

You reach the brown Hudson sedan, more than a decade old, now, its round, old-fashioned rump gleaming in the afternoon sun, its windows cracked slightly for air. You and your sister scramble into the Hudson's back seat and grab at the wide sateen travel pouch before you. In this, you stow your rubber bathing caps and flip flops, alongside the card games and crayons left

from the annual August vacation in the Smoky Mountains. You don't color any more—you're eleven—but on car trips, you like to regress a little, drawing cartoon characters with giant heads, mashing them against the windows so people in passing cars can see. Now Mommy, who you've been getting up the courage to call Mom, as teenagers would do, starts the car, and soon you're gliding north on A1A, past Lauderdale-by-the-Sea, past gated Sea Ranch Lakes, to the left-hand turn into Bel-Air, its concrete sign painted white with raised aqua letters, flanked by plantings of red flowering hibiscus and croton, their green, red, and yellow tongue-leaves jostling each time a car turns in.

One day in the future, you'll visit Hawaii and imagine you've come home, and you'll think of how the end of your childhood in south Florida coincided with the first swell of your breasts, and with the day you and your mother and sister swerved into the gravel driveway of 1961 SE Sixteenth Court to meet Daddy, home from the insurance office, home with the news you were moving in two weeks to a small fishing and citrus town halfway up the coast, a wide-spot-in-the-road none of your classmates, transplanted Northerners like you, have ever heard of, a deeply Southern town called Titusville, which, you'd find out, had recently designated itself "The Gateway to the Galaxies."

Mom and Dad undoubtedly discussed the move together, but it would have been his idea. She once said that was the way it went: he'd brood about some major decision for days or weeks or months, turning it over and over in his mind, and one day announce his plan. After the shock of it, she'd cross-examine him: Have you thought of this? Of that? And always, he had thought of everything, down to the last detail, and the plan was air-tight, and usually wise. His ingrown intelligence. His prac-ticed self-reliance. Recently, a family historian described the McCutchan temperament as "self-contained, private but not repressed, highly focused," and my understanding of him deep-ened, though I admit that, so many years after his death, I could be making parts of him up.

And I wonder, was this self-containment, this reticence, this kind of humility, not a character trait of "The Greatest Generation"? The historian added: "McCutchans are verbal, sometimes eloquent—but will not give up secrets, or even 'the information.' Also, their focus drives them to see things to the end—and then some. Many are given to wanderlust." That last one I seem to have inherited, myself.

Our move from Washington to south Florida had been exciting, but with the Titusville move, something seemed to be off—there was no twirl around the kitchen. The reasons for leaving, some of which I might have understood at eleven, had they been laid out, were muddled. In sad tones, I told my sixth grade teacher and classmates I'd be gone soon. "We're moving," I said, lowering my head, as if I were guilty of something. Worse was surrendering my rented clarinet to the beginning band director. I'd just started playing the instrument, and though I'd picked it because a friend had and I wanted to sit next to her, it already felt like part of my body. So are significant choices occasionally made.

We sold the sandy old Hudson to a retired neighbor for fifty dollars. The jolly couple next door with the Arthur Godfrey record collection and the fat yellow dog named Gin threw us a farewell dinner. Estalene and I bid good-bye to our favorite playmates, the Foglia girls across the street, daughters of Bel-Air's developer, who, during hurricanes, were permitted to race outside, tie a long rope to their station wagon door and hold tight to the line, screaming with feral joy, as the wind whipped them back and forth in the driveway.

One day, three men and a Mayflower truck collected our furniture, and we loaded clothes, linens, and kitchen supplies into a small U-Haul hooked to the orange and white Fairlane with the rocket tailfins. On the morning we left, Mom drove, I sat next to her, and Estalene took the backseat with our games and books. Just us three, Daddy's girls. He'd gone ahead on his own.

As we crept out of Bel-Air, the U-Haul bucked a little on the numbered asphalt lanes, courts, and terraces, so we slowed down, past the overchlorinated community swimming pool, where I'd learned to dive, badly, and the deep, undeveloped thicket across from it, where I'd wandered by myself among pines festooned with morning glories, their purple faces intermittently split by sunbeams shooting through. I gazed at my private retreat, then sideways at my mother, who was uncharacteristically quiet at the start of an outing, and noticed her cheeks were wet.

What Mom wept over was too private to question, for she rarely shed tears, but I assumed she was sad to leave. Of the four of us, she had engaged most intentionally with the south Florida landscape, saving the best of our seashell finds in a velvety green box. She had been the first of us to poke at a Portuguese man-of-war washed up on the beach, its wavy, venomous tentacles spreading from the balloon-like bladder that once floated on the ocean's surface. She had followed the seasons of the giant sea turtles that, during the warmer months, nested on the beach, would round us up in the middle of the night to go turtle watching with friends and neighbors. In the Hudson, we advanced toward the ocean, low beams only, and from the parking lot, stepped carefully, toes first into the sand, so as not to make a sound. Finding the others, we waited in the dark until someone detected the soft, slow scrape of a loggerhead's shell on wet meal, and silently moved toward it. We could just make out the turtle's dome-like carapace as she ambulated up from shore, hauling herself to a dry spot to begin scooping a nest with her rear flippers. The sand flew. By now, one or two in our group had trained a flashlight on the turtle's backside; she was deep into her ritual, oblivious to us, and eventually she lowered herself into the fresh cradle and deposited her eggs—dozens of them, like ping-pong balls. Finished, the mother turtle kicked sand over her brood and lumbered back to the sea.

Having come to south Florida so young, Estalene and I took its beauty, its subtle seasons, for granted, while our mother had arrived as a committed explorer. Was this what Mom would miss? Or was she mourning her job, her friends? By the time we hit US 1, the coastal highway, she seemed to have recovered, chatting about the adventure ahead. She was wired for optimism, for looking forward to what comes next, imagining the good anything would lead to. In my mother lay the confidence that everything in the universe was somehow connected, and all you had to do was step into its marvelous web, contribute your share of energy, and marvel at the surprises and opportunities certain to come your way.

((((((

Eight months earlier, February 1962, John Glenn had become the first American to orbit Earth—not just once, but three times. During those five hours, the world stayed tuned as Glenn, traveling high above at 17,000 miles per hour, watched the sun set and rise, radioing in his awe. All of Perth, Australia, turned on its lights as Glenn passed over; he saw the glow, the outline of a city. A revolutionary perspective: Earth as a fascinating object, a blue ball of land and water viewed from afar, whose twenty-four-hour day suddenly seemed less than a blip of time. At once, a human's position in the universe was either enlarged or diminished, depending on how one interpreted the view.

I didn't understand the consequences of Glenn's mission then. I was enthralled because the astronaut was blonde and handsome and charismatic, and his craft, *Friendship 7*, was named for a peaceful human attribute, not a faraway constellation or a patriotic symbol. He'd orbited the earth more than once, beyond the call of duty, it seemed, making him a magnificent overachiever. And yet, as he emerged triumphant from his capsule, removing his white helmet for the photographers and the television audience, he was just the nicest guy you'd ever want to meet.

What prompted my father to pull us out of school seven months after John Glenn's orbits and drag or spirit us up the coast is all conjecture. But the national situation and Dad's personal history suggest possible motives.

In September, President Kennedy delivered his famous Moon Speech at Rice University Stadium in Houston, a few miles north of the new Manned Spacecraft Center. It was JFK's more public vow, sure to be well received, now that John Glenn had demonstrated America's powerful technology, had witnessed that extraordinary view of Earth from Space, and shown, by inference, America's ability to dominate it.

The nation was ready and eager to listen, prepared by a clever marketing strategy. In a reversal of standard military secrecy, NASA had issued generous previews of impending missions, giving *Life* magazine an exclusive contract for personal stories about the astronauts and their families. The original seven had appeared on a cover in 1959, their wives the following week. "Astronauts' Wives: Their Inner Thoughts, Worries," the teaser promised, above the proud support team in boat-neck blouses and crimson lipstick.

In Houston, those surrounding the youngest president were mostly men, dressed, as he was, in dark suits, white shirts, and ties, faces reddening under the open sky, fanning themselves with paper programs, a few sweating it out under ten-gallon hats. Vice President Lyndon Johnson, for whom the Houston center would one day be renamed, sat behind President

Kennedy, to the right, one elbow cocked on an armrest, his fist pressed into his cheek. He and everyone around him, especially those in dark sunglasses, looked mad or suspicious, but that's what happens to your face under the intense southern sun, when the only defenses you have are shades and your eyebrows.

In his opening remarks, President Kennedy said,

> We meet in an hour of change and challenge, in a decade of hope and fear, in an age of both knowledge and ignorance. The greater our knowledge increases, the greater our ignorance unfolds.
>
> Despite the striking fact that most of the scientists that the world has ever known are alive and working today, despite the fact that this Nation's own scientific manpower is doubling every 12 years in a rate of growth more than three times that of our population as a whole, despite that, the vast stretches of the unknown and the unanswered and the unfinished still far outstrip our collective comprehension.

The message was clear: Americans were great, but in danger of falling behind. We must persevere and triumph in the Space Race, the Cold War.

Then Kennedy put a dizzying spin on that message, collapsing history—as Glenn's feat had collapsed time—so suddenly and completely one felt strapped to a blazing comet. It was impossible to hop off, now.

> No man can fully grasp how far and how fast we have come, but condense, if you will, the 50,000 years of man's recorded history in a time span of but a half a century. . . . About 10 years ago, under this standard, man emerged

from his caves to construct other kinds of shelter. Only five
years ago man learned to write and use a cart with wheels.
Christianity began less than two years ago. The printing
press came this year, and then less than two months ago
. . . the steam engine provided a new source of power.
. . . Last month electric lights and telephones and auto-
mobiles and airplanes became available. Only last week did
we develop penicillin and television and nuclear power,
and now if America's new spacecraft succeeds in reaching
Venus, we will have literally reached the stars before midnight tonight.

It was the rhetoric of the motivational speaker, an arms gathering, a rousing hymn to action, familiar and dear to all Americans since the first colonial Bible thumping. We had conquered
our own country once upon a time, and now, by way of a moonquest, we would conquer another, and perhaps two: the Soviet
Union, and Outer Space. Plus, we would reap advances in education, science and technology, and jobs. The vehicle: "a giant
rocket more than 300 feet tall, the length of this football field,
made of new metal alloys, some of which have not yet been
invented, capable of standing heat and stresses several times
more than have ever been experienced, fitted together with a
precision better than the finest watch, carrying all the equip-
ment needed for propulsion, guidance, control, communica-
tions, food and survival, on an untried mission, to an unknown
celestial body."

Who would not cheer the image of a colossal Saturn V
rocket heaved upward with an oil field's worth of jet fuel, a
spaceship so huge it would require its own building for assembly, that building so vast it would have its own weather system?
Who would not be spellbound by the idea of accomplishing this

in a mere seven years? It was, even to those suspicious of over-blown rhetoric, of politics, a glorious moment. It was the future; it was science fiction come to pass, the story launched on a Flor-ida beach.

((((((

On October 14 an American U-2 flew over Cuba and returned with photos of Soviet nuclear weapons. On the fifteenth, the worst standoff between the United States and the Soviet Union ensued, with the very real threat of nuclear war. Yet we didn't know we were vulnerable until October 22, when the president, in a televised address, announced there were Soviet missiles in Cuba. By then, the armed forces were mobilizing.

"I remember as a teenager watching all the trains come through town, loaded with tanks," an elderly state archivist and Marianna, Florida, native told me one afternoon, as I tried to divine my father's motive to leave a good job and go up to Titus-ville. "Everyone was scared—especially the old-timers, the ones who served in World War II." A friend who grew up on the Gulf Coast near Tampa described the barbed wire coiled up and down the beaches. "All the kids were freaked out," he said.

The crisis ended on the twenty-eighth, when Nikita Khrush-chev announced he had ordered the Soviet missile bases in Cuba removed. Analysts still debate the private exchanges between Khrushchev and Kennedy, but public reaction to the crisis, especially in Florida, had been pure fright. Would Flor-ida have taken Russia's opening volley? It's hard to say. The mis-siles rumored to be perched on high alert in Cuba could have hit nearly any US city in minutes. As with the 9/11 catastrophe, New York or Washington might sooner have drawn the enemy's sight. But those closest to Havana imagined they'd be first.

A few days later, Mom and Dad said we were moving, and

in two weeks we were out of Bel-Air, arriving in Titusville in time to feel the ground-shaking boom of a Saturn I rocket test, see frightened birds erupt from trees. We celebrated Thanksgiving with an improvised feast in our rented duplex or possibly fried clams and peppermint stick ice cream at Howard Johnson's, the fanciest restaurant in town, by the Indian River, the long waterway—a saltwater sound—separating the town from Merritt Island and the Space Center. Dad would have wanted to treat us, lift our sad, angry, bewildered spirits.

But was his decision to move borne of the missile crisis? As my father's daughter, I think it may have been a contributing factor, but not the whole story. I say Dad had been brooding on it since the year before, when the president promised we'd land a man on the moon by the end of the 1960s. The postwar economy was still healthy; there would be, he probably thought, a good climate for new business ventures. He watched as the Space Coast villages began to grow, imagined a jump out of the corporate world to an independent business in a boomtown. After the Moon Speech in September, and the averted crisis in October, he decided the time was ripe, and we left our tropical home, a growing urban scene populated by Yankees like us. On November 26, Brevard County's records say, my sister and I entered the Titusville schools. Our Fort Lauderdale transcripts, an afterthought, arrived from Broward County in December.

❨ ❨ ❨

Central Avenue, Titusville, was a short dirt road bushwhacked out of a mess of scrub palmetto and vines for no other reason than to throw up a line of identical concrete block duplexes— indeed, the two-bedroom semi-furnished unit Dad rented for us at number 305 was painted the same weary taupe as its three flat-roofed companions. It had no gutters, and when it rained,

water spilled off the roof straight into the sand and scrawny
bushes beneath the windows, splashing up against the homely
exterior, leaving a residue of dirt and leaves, and a loamy smell
I would always associate with the town. We were familiar, of
course, with block housing. Our ranch home in Fort Lauderdale had been assembled on a concrete slab of concrete blocks,
with no siding masking the simple materials, and like millions
of these "little dugans" (as Dad called them) in the Sunshine
State, painted contractor white with primary or pastel trim and
surrounded by bright hibiscus plantings. But the drab duplex
on Central Avenue had none of that tropical cheer—not even
one of those screened front doors with the tin egret tacked into
the frame. It looked to me like army facilities, and might as well
have been. After all, we were now participating in a war.

During World War II, the government had plopped 172 military installations onto the Florida peninsula, and one of them,
Banana River Naval Air Station, Cape Canaveral, became the
platform for the country's space missions. The military had
used concrete blocks for years, for foxholes and temporary shelters, the idea stretching back to 1906, the year Thomas Edi-
son, visionary, sometime Florida resident, and proud owner of a
new cement plant announced, "I am going to live to see the day
when a working man's house can be built of concrete in a week.
. . . If I succeed, it will take from the city slums everybody who
is worth taking." When the winter-white flight to sunny Florida
commenced after the war, builders looking for cheap, easy construction may have looked to military bases for inspiration. And
why not? Concrete didn't attract termites, or support mold and
mildew. It stood up to hurricane-force winds and was fire resistant. Thus the entire state of Florida, a sheet of sand and humus
floating on perforated limestone and water, erupted with above-
ground bunkers, cooled by way of hand-cranked windows and

decorated with more concrete: circular driveways, flower boxes, birdbaths from which chalk-white cherubs, flip-tailed fish, or purse-lipped bathing beauties burbled ardently oxygenated water.

❨ ❨ ❨

The evening Mom and Estalene and I turned into the muddy dun of Central Avenue, we felt we had arrived in reduced circumstances. Titusville, caught off guard by President Kennedy's vow to land a man on the moon, was short on housing, and Dad had been lucky to snag 305, while other newcomers camped out in motels and trailer parks, some for months. One family we knew, coming down from Jacksonville, stayed an hour from Titusville at a relative's lake house that, though equipped with a toilet, had no tub or hot water; through the better part of a summer, as their new home was completed, everyone bathed in the lake.

Our neighbors on Central Avenue were NASA employees on temporary or long-term assignment, all awaiting the opening of a new housing development—an Orange Park, a Sunny Isles, or a more pretentious Royal Palm Estates. The young family across the communal scrap of Saint Augustine grass we called a yard consisted of an engineer, his wife, and their blond, three-year-old daughter Susan, who introduced herself as Sue-Tu-un and spent the afternoons swinging on a tire a previous tenant had strung from a hackberry. The Wilsons, Alabama natives, had moved down from Huntsville, their speech asway with diphthongs; they were the first real Southerners I had ever met. Their hometown had been the site of the Redstone Arsenal during World War II and was transformed as headquarters for the army's missile research program when German rocket scientist Wernher von Braun and his colleagues were brought over via Operation Paperclip. The Marshall Space Flight Center, where Mr. Wilson had worked, opened in 1960.

Moving into 305 took no more than a day. The place offered mismatched but serviceable furniture; ours would remain in storage until Dad could get us into one of the new neighborhoods. From the U-Haul, we pulled our necessities, and I remember some internal excitement—just like camping!—but mostly, a gloomy foreboding and anxious questions that grew tall, then askew, like the beaten shrubs by the front door. Why did we have to stay in such an ugly place? How would we live in half the space we'd known? Where would I get any privacy?

One morning I woke up in my twin bed, three feet across from my dozing sister, and discovered a flare of blood across the New England crazy quilt we'd brought for a touch of Mom's heritage. I inspected my knees—had I skinned one, and not noticed? I crept out to the little hallway, found the bathroom free, locked myself in on the toilet, and peered down in the water. So that's what it was. I'd been waiting, hoping for it, but the booklets Mom had given me two years before (You're a Young Lady Now; Very Personally Yours) were no preparation for how it looked: red blossoms floating, wavering, like low-tide creatures I'd once gazed upon in Key West. I found the elastic and cotton contraption and pulled it on. But I wouldn't tell anyone. I couldn't—we were all too close, and too distracted. I would get too much attention, or none at all, and the thought of either extreme—and in that transitory state, I was always thinking in extremes—made me want to cry. For four months I stored the used pads in my bottom drawer, tucked like fat snails, sneaking them out to the garbage in a grocery sack when no one was home.

On a rainy afternoon, Mom quietly took me aside. Perhaps she had been putting clothes away in my dresser, sniffed the sour musk of those pads. "Sweetie, I don't believe I told you how to dispose of used ones," she said. "Let me show you." And she did, and to my relief, we didn't speak of it again.

II

The linear velocity of Earth's surface is greatest toward the equa-
tor, and since Florida is the closest state to that 0-degree belt,
it made sense to stage prograde—moving in the same direction as the Earth's rotation—launches there. Think of the best
spot for jumping on a merry-go-round in the direction the ride
is going. And although Cape Canaveral is well north of, say, Key
West, the long, stringy barrier island, 15,000 acres of sand and
scrub, had other advantages. The area downrange of the cape
was lightly populated; accidents there would endanger few people, and if a launch failed, the ocean likely would catch whatever plummeted. As well, a launch over water was less observable
than a launch over land—a plus for secret missions. Too, the
cape lay far south of busy transatlantic air routes, and islands in
the South Atlantic and West Indies offered good tracking sites.

So the cape, previously accessible only by boat and occupied
by a scant handful of settlers who fished, hunted, grew oranges,
or ran mom-and-pop fishing camps, became, in the late 1940s,
a ballistic missile testing range under the auspices of the US
Army, Navy, and Air Force, and in the early 1950s, the base
for manned spacecraft launches. By 1961, NASA announced it
would acquire north and west of the launch area about 88,000
acres, including working citrus groves, small communities,
and newer housing developments. Of 440 tracts, three-fourths
were owned by absentees, including wealthy industrialists outside Florida who used the land as private hunting preserves. (On
the site of the current launch control pad once stood a Har-
vard club, furnished with wicker chairs, Audubon prints, and
a thick ledger of birds and animals bagged. According to a former postman out there, the members had their favorite bread

flown in daily.) Distant investors could negotiate with ease, but locals who had built homes, schools, and businesses on their property had a hard time. They didn't want to leave ancestral ground, the government's offers were low-ball, the time frame was too narrow, and where were they supposed to move, when housing on the mainland was so tight? Protest meetings ensued, to little effect. A friend whose grandparents were forced off their property remembers one longtime cracker who briefly held off government agents with a shotgun—and he was probably not the only one. The man's house, a rough structure with a bare concrete floor, was immediately bulldozed, while others lay untouched for a while; according to a friend who worked at the cape, top dogs used them for extramarital trysts. The grandparents' house, a newer two-story, the dream retirement home they had saved for, NASA used for a medical infirmary until the day it, too, was cleared away.

What land NASA didn't directly use became in 1963 the Merritt Island National Wildlife Refuge, which, like other nature refuges adjacent to military installations, served as a buffer, a modern-day moat.

(((

Although supposedly dedicated to peacetime scientific research, NASA's participation in the Space Race was decidedly warlike. Three waves of troops arrived, the first in 1959 supporting Project Mercury, the man-in-space initiative. In a blink, hundreds of engineers, scientists, and other personnel flocked to the Cape Canaveral area, bringing families to communities like Titusville and its sisters on the southern end of Brevard County: Cocoa, Merritt Island, and Melbourne. In 1961, Project Gemini, dedicated to longer flights, space rendezvous techniques, and perfected landings, attracted the second wave of troops. Project Apollo, the moonquest, also begun in 1961, was responsible for the third surge.

When our family showed up we were not on the ground floor, but many arrived after we did, and some who'd already come soon departed for assignments in Texas, California, and other places where aircraft were fabricated, personnel were trained, flights were tracked. The concept of Manifest Destiny, the push to expand west across the continent, was comparatively simple: you started on the East Coast, where your forebears landed—mine in 1620s Maine and 1830s New York—and, depending on how late you arrived, kept moving in a straight line until you reached new territory and claimed it. But in central Florida, nobody was operating on such a continuum—and to be honest, no one in Florida ever had; movement, in and out, has been the state's single constant. To put the cape's situation visually, so much darting in and away created a starred effect, emblematic of the collective imagination's goal. In gunning for the moon, all systems go, we would fracture time and space into points, a star polygon, not a closed circle or linear path.

We would fracture our social structures, too, or at least lie vulnerable to the instability swift change brings. During those years, a lot of modern snake oilers passed through, tricking the dazed and dislocated with promises, lies. I wasn't surprised to learn that for a time in the 1960s, Brevard County led the nation in divorce and venereal disease, results of transient living. For six months, Titusville supported a diet doctor who dispensed worthless pills to fat teens. My mother and I were among his victims; as my figure rounded noticeably on Neapolitan ice cream, Krispy Kreme doughnuts, and Zero bars, she, tired of nagging me, placed me in the hands of he who I'll call Dr. No, a fiftyish gent from the northeast, who, himself fat, weighed me weekly and adjusted my pill intake—more of the blue pills, fewer of the pink, and this week, add two yellow. His office, in one of the featureless, hastily nailed up business strips, was divided into three examination stalls by plastic shower curtains. Out front, the waiting room accommodated several molded chairs, and here, I occasionally ran into fellow fatties from school, girls as embarrassed as I was to be there. Once Dr. No was outed (for the pills were very sweet, and no one lost weight), he skipped town overnight.

Into another part of town waltzed a handsome new Baptist youth minister with dark wavy hair, a poet's name, and connections to the Campus Crusade for Christ, an evangelical organization attractive to both Titusville's religious conservatives and untethered newcomers seeking an anchor. Historically, the CCC was associated with the neo-Pentecostal Charismatic movement, led in part by five south Florida men known as the Fort Lauderdale Five. I had a good chuckle when I discovered Titusville had once been home to the Florida Song Book Company, publisher of *A Messenger for Jesus*, a 1913 hymnbook you could buy by the dozen for $3.60, postage paid. That is the only music publication in the Library of Congress's entire collection associated with Titusville. But I digress. In the 1960s, old-school Pentecostals and new Charismatics found common ground in ecstatic tongues and prophecies, and this new youth minister, part of the swirl, was, in current parlance, a rock star; if memory serves, he played the guitar. Even TV actor Michael Landon's appearance at Florida Wonderland, Titusville's crude tourist attraction, didn't draw a crowd as large as the mob of young women desperately seeking saving by the handsome minister; the craze for *Jesus Christ Superstar* probably fanned the flames (Estalene and Mom got the album; when the opening strains leaped out of the Magnavox stereo, I fled to my room, a musical snob, suspicious of pop-Christ's appeal). After the fellow left, rumors flew: he had deflowered a few of the most adoring converts, some said. A long time afterward, a high school friend confessed to me she had submitted to him.

《 《 《

Because church is the primary—and often the only—entryway to a Southern community, we joined Titusville First Methodist immediately, standing to be recognized at the eleven o'clock service, signing up for Sunday school, which I declared I'd outgrown—and after a year or so, and many family discussions thick with pleading and whining, it was decided that, forget Sunday school, eleven o'clock was enough for everyone. Thus we established our Sabbath morning routine, all of us resisting it to degrees we had not in Fort Lauderdale. I can hear the toaster's hiccups, the shower's whish, bureau drawers yanked out and slammed shut, cries of "Who's got the deodorant?" and "I can't go—I have a run in my hose!" Always, something had to be ironed at the last minute, somebody couldn't find their Good Purse, and even Dad might lope down the hall, muttering, "No black socks." We often arrived too late to park in First Methodist's lot, wound up down the street by a decrepit frame house quaking with tropical overgrowth and had to scamper over broken concrete to the sanctuary, where we hovered in the narthex, waiting to be seated after the opening prayer and hymn. As the organist leaned in to the closing chords, we were ushered swiftly to a back row, like concertgoers who've dawdled irresponsibly at dinner and missed the first movement.

The sanctuary was rather plain and overwhelmingly tan, like the inside of a cardboard box, so the eye was instantly drawn to the large stained glass window high up in back of the choir, picturing Jesus in a red cloak, holding a lamb. The altar was brack-

eted by a wooden rail, at which, the year I was confirmed and
kneeled to pledge my life to Christ, I silently pledged my life to
Music, for since my epiphany at Calvin Christian Day School,
I had not sought a center in religion, but in art and nature,
though religious context and material served as vehicles, and
often intertwined with them.

First Methodist's decor may have lacked inspiration, but in
the pulpit was Reverend Ed Norman with the jug ears and a
soft, raised gaze that never focused on any individual, yet gathered listeners, as if by peering past us, he led us. He loved music,
too, and kept a trumpet in the pulpit, lifting it to play along on
his favorite hymns, politely stepping aside of the microphone to
do it. At a time when magazines asked if God was dead, Reverend Norman's earnest trumpet playing seemed proof that He
wasn't. Behind the reverend, the chancel choir starred not one,
but two operatic sopranos, probably rocket scientists' wives
who'd once sung in San Francisco or Stuttgart and, finding
Titusville wanting in the arts, drew satisfaction from battling it
out every Sunday in church. It was clear to everyone that Mrs.
Womack and Mrs. Stoutamire were meant for better things
(especially Mrs. Womack), and though they added body to the
choir sound, they couldn't blend (especially Mrs. Womack),
and when Mrs. Womack and Mrs. Stoutamire sang duets at the
Christmas Eve service, you could see the veins popping out on
Mrs. Womack's forehead, all the way up in the balcony.

A town whose social life revolved around church activities
was new to us. In Fort Lauderdale, we had merely attended Sunday school and services, Mom and Dad switching churches and
denominations every few years, searching for good sermons, not,
particularly, community. To my knowledge, neither had served
a church there past the white envelope flipped into the collection
plate every Sunday, the single exception being the time Mom

volunteered for the Living Manger Scene outside Lighthouse Point Presbyterian. At five feet eleven, she was cast as one of the Three Wise Men, and for several balmy, December evenings she stood silently at the back of the palm-shaded tableau in a long robe and turban, holding forth a gold painted box that had once been a Whitman's Sampler. Dad, Estalene, and I drove by to gently heckle her, but she remained in character, her face trained on a manger overflowing with Spanish moss, within which lay the rubber Christ Child.

Dad served on the church finance committee, and Mom dropped in on a women's prayer group that gave thanks at the beach. It was what they needed to do, and they didn't begrudge it. (Here I stop and ask, how did I spring from such even-tempered people? I'd already heard about another girl's mother hooked on lithium, a father who drank too much and yelled at the TV. These stories horrified me; maybe they weren't even true.) Soon after a disastrous try at the local Girl Scout troop, Mom suggested I join the Methodist Youth Fellowship, an idea I repeatedly rejected until one Sunday afternoon when she begged and then demanded that I go, for she knew I was having trouble adjusting to Titusville and needed a group, any group. I acquiesced in tears, weeping and snuffling all the way to church, glaring at her as she let me out, stomping into the Fellowship Hall, flushed and sullen. Inside, on a just-mopped linoleum floor, several smiling kids bounced a ball around, preparing to play Four Square. I recoiled, not knowing anyone, judging the game to be stupid. Yet I had no choice but to be nice and join in, for even an introvert knows sociability has advantages, and I enjoyed myself.

I stuck with the MYF through the fall, dreaming up a Halloween creep show fund-raiser that sent blindfolded church members crawling through a maze of spaghetti guts and grape eye-

balls, while somebody's little brother played a 45-rpm record of
The Monster Mash over and over. But I stopped attending in the
spring, after several of us traveled to a Methodist youth camp in
another part of the state. Instead of tents in the Okeechobee wild,
we twelve- and thirteen-year-olds were assigned cinder block huts
on mowed acreage, and I drew one full of girls far more Southern
and churchy than I could possibly pretend to be. Unsure of how
to fit in, I floated, wraith-like, in and out of group activities—
swimming, nature walks, campfire hymn singing. Residuals from
that week include the lusty mess hall mantra—Apple butter, peanut butter, butter butter!—citing the camp's basic condiments,
provided in pale green Melmac bowls at every table.

But what stuck with me, and haunts me still, was the terrible predicament of the camper assigned to the bunk beneath
mine. The girl, who, like me, knew no one else in the cabin,
wet her bed every night; by morning, the ammonia stench
had risen to my pillow and I lay there, wondering if I needed
do something about it. During the day, the girl's sheets were
silently exchanged, but the smell inside the cabin persisted and
thickened, as the other girls gathered in twitchy groups, giggling and exclaiming over the poor camper's problem. "How
can y'all stand it?" they cried out when I walked by, and I felt
caught between what felt like a social pressure to be catty, the
need to crack a merciful joke, fear of being associated with the
smell, and the pity I felt for my bunkmate. I would sit with her
at meals, making small talk, for she was shy and embarrassed
and probably suffered from a malady I couldn't imagine. But I
was inconsistent about it, lacking the courage to declare myself
the girl's friend or protector, loitering in the vicinity of the gossipy ones when they went off to swim, leaving the troubled girl
behind. What did it mean, anyway, to be "my brother's keeper?"
Whatever it was, I made a halfhearted effort, and failed.

《 《 《

When we got to Titusville, the whole town was on fire. Fire in the ditches, fire in the vacant lots, fire in the rickety, ubiquitous pines. Central Florida is the lightning capital of the world, someone told us, and Titusville is the eastern, Atlantic terminus of what's known as Lightning Alley, a stretch running west to Tampa on the Gulf. I remember the lightning, which seemed to pop at random. Large storms generated tens of thousands of cloud-to-ground strikes, sizzling fingers, zapping at angles. Something was always smoldering around there. Lightning fires seemed not to spread, though some did. Frequent showers doused most of them, leaving sandlots and ditches smoking under the clearing sky. You simply stepped or drove around a chip of flame or plume of ash, the way you'd avoid a crack on the sidewalk, or roadkill. It wasn't unusual to catch sight of a dying fire on the walk to or from my new school, Parkway Junior High. The trudge always left me damp with sweat and obsessed with my current, and always limp, hairdo, sprayed with enough Aqua Net to attract and entrap the occasional fly or mosquito. Often I walked into light, localized rainfall and out again, as if I'd passed under the arc of a lawn sprinkler. By the time I got to school, my clothes smelled like ozone and cinders.

I often wished Titusville had enough streets to offer an alternative path to school, but it did not. At least the way was completely paved. Plastic purse slung over my shoulder, new clarinet case in one hand and books crooked in the opposite arm, I crossed busy Garden Street to Forell Avenue, to which a pair of horseshoe streets, Lilac Circle and Eden Circle, were joined. From there, I passed over Tropic Avenue and continued on aptly named Rock Pit Road, so coined for a swimming hole where "fast" teens reportedly earned the wages of sin, but which I never saw. At South Street, I hung a left and shambled down to Parkway, at the corner of South and Park. Across South stood a shopping center anchored by W. T. Grant's, a chain dime store that sold buckets and mops, pet goldfish and mice, Evening in Paris perfume, and, lying flat on a wooden table, cones pointing proudly to the ceiling, padded bras, which a husky girl I knew liked to punch down with her fists. Sometimes after school, a friend and I would walk across to Grant's for french fries and Cokes in its yellow restaurant and talk about all the boys we had crushes on and what kind of kissers they might be. Once, as we mooned over our imagined choices, there was a grease fire in the kitchen, and the manager sprayed it with a white substance as the woman in a hairnet flipping burgers tossed a few new patties on the grill.

❨ ❨ ❨

Like any other respectable Florida community, Titusville had a ticketed tourist attraction, the brainchild of Mr. and Mrs. H. C. Kirk who had, three years prior to our move, cleared, gouged, and reconfigured 101 acres on South US 1 to create Florida Wonderland. A latecomer in the genre, Florida Wonderland was doomed to close by 1973, and not just because Disney World had opened thirty miles away. The place was, thematically speaking, a mess, offering a Monkey Jungle, a Seminole Indian village, western gunfights, and an "animated fairyland." There was a Ferris wheel and a snake house, a Jungle Queen train and a stagecoach hold-up every twenty minutes. There was a pygmy elephant that waterskied, a spitting cobra, an alligator, and a chimpanzee that wore silly hats and pretended to talk on a phone. Florida Wonderland's first brochure contained a photograph of the once-forested site, predevelopment, with the caption: "This is the forest primeval. Raw jungle from which Florida Wonderland was carved by man and machine."

In an adjacent shot, the visionaries responsible, Mr. and Mrs. Kirk, "relax beneath one of the giant oaks along the trail" in pith helmet sunhats. But an aerial photo of the attraction seems devoid of oaks, dominated instead by a giant parking lot, various western-style buildings, acres of lawn sliced by service roads, and a few stands of the original palmetto palms, which presumably shaded the trail leading to the Wild West "hanging tree."

We tried Florida Wonderland once, when the actor Michael Landon, who played Little Joe on the popular TV western *Bonanza*, made an appearance, flying in from Orlando in a tiny plane. I vaguely recall his entrance on an outdoor platform behind the concrete mermaid, and the invitation to climb the steps for his autograph (I hung back). That is all. No one in the McCutchan family cared for staged shoot-outs or phony nature rides. Besides, we'd seen better in Miami. Far more interesting were later accounts of monkeys escaping into nearby housing developments, and the sad news that Wanda the elephant slipped her chain in the parking lot, tried to cross US 1, and got hit by a truck.

In 1965, the Olympic swimmer and Hollywood actor Johnny Weissmuller, a.k.a. Tarzan, retired to Florida and either invested in or "endorsed" the attraction depending on who you talk to. Either way, it was renamed Johnny Weissmuller's Tropical/Florida Wonderland, also called Tarzan's Jungleland. Yet the graying star failed to add sufficient luster to the place, and by the time it closed, it was said, one could see more of the original birds, reptiles, and animals outside the park than within it.

❨ ❨ ❨

In Fort Lauderdale I had been a model Brownie Scout, daughter of a veteran, given the privilege, at nine, of leading the Brownie Scout Promise at a rally from the broadcast booth of a high school football stadium. The *Sun-Sentinel*, hard up for artwork that week, ran my photo, holding up the two-fingered salute, promising to do my best. During one summer trip back to Maine, I attended the same scout camp my mother had enjoyed when she was young, and, with a hardy group of girls hailing from Portland, Presque Isle, and Millinocket, triumphantly followed the trail she'd once hiked up Mount Katahdin. I corresponded with two of my Maine friends for more than a year; I kept my camp woodworking project, a missile-shaped ornament of heart pine, until I went to college.

But as I approached my eleventh birthday, I grew suspicious of good-girl, community-minded activity. I canceled my subscription to the Scout magazine *American Girl* and stopped wearing my uniform to school on troop meeting days. My mother noticed the latter immediately. "What's the matter?" she asked. "Are you *ashamed* of your Girl Scout uniform?"

To be ashamed of my uniform meant being ashamed of her. I couldn't admit to that. "It's in the laundry," I'd say, or, "We're doing arts and crafts and I don't want to mess it up." But inside, I was screaming, "Yes! Yes! I'm ashamed of my Girl Scout uniform! I don't WANT to wear a uniform, of any kind, *ever*."

It was not just adolescent rebellion, but the emergence of a natural detachment I'd never shake. I was more introverted, more bookish, than my mother; I needed privacy for my own projects, inspired, perhaps, by art, nature, or a like-minded friend or two. To this day, people mistake my social engagement for extraversion, when I am really often occupying the artist's position: partly immersed in life, partly observing or commenting on it.

We fought over the uniform for the better part of 1962, and when we moved to Titusville I hoped my connection to scouting would break naturally—perhaps the town was too small for a troop. But to my dismay, my mother found one, joined me up, and accepted the leader's invitation to accompany a dozen eleven-year-olds on a camping trip by a lake and orange grove. Mom's skills—blazing trails, building fires, crafting sturdy lean-tos out of limbs and vines she'd torn from the forest—were touted in preparatory meetings.

The camping trip turned out to be a wimpy one-nighter. On a chilly Saturday afternoon, we drove to the edge of the grove and hiked past the freeze-ready smudge pots less than a mile to a pond. There, we were grouped in twos and threes and instructed to pitch our tents. As Mrs. McCutchan's daughter, I was assigned a tent with two older "helping" scouts: the troop leader's precocious daughter, Lindy, a gypsy-eyed girl of thirteen, and an even older girl, Margie, fifteen, who had short red hair and volunteered as a Candy Striper in the local hospital. Also helping out were three Eagle Scouts in their late teens, camped a discreet quarter-mile away. We were, after all, in the South, where it was assumed that even women like my mother needed male protection.

After the campfire meal of hamburger stew and s'mores, the swampland ghost stories and the doleful singing of "Kumbaya," we shuffled off to our tents, flashlights sweeping the ground for snakes. I wriggled into my sleeping bag right away, but Lindy and Margie sat on top of theirs, fiddling with a wind-up alarm clock.

"They want midnight," Margie said. "So we get to sleep for two hours."

"What?" I said.

"Midnight," said Lindy. "That's when we're meeting the boys. You have to come, too. Three of them, three of us."

"But you could get in trouble," I said, horrified.

"If you're with us, no one will tell," Margie said.

I wasn't about to challenge the older girls. I was new to the group, and, as my mother's daughter, regarded with suspicion. A possible goody-goody. I didn't want that reputation, but neither did I want to be, or be thought, a bad girl. I accepted my entrapment, hoping the plan would fall through.

At midnight the clock buzzed, rousing Lindy and Margie, who had actually slept. They pulled on their shirts and shorts and scooted out of the tent. "Come on!" they hissed. "The boys are waiting!"

I dawdled, asking if they really wanted me along.

"Yes! Yes!" they hissed again.

We took to the path without flashlights, heading deeper into the woods, toward a flickering fire. The boys greeted Lindy and Margie like partners in crime. "And who is this?" a dark-haired fellow asked, looking at me.

"This is Ann," Lindy said. "Ain't she bitchin'?"

I cringed. I was not bitchin'; I was a skag. It was true that I'd already grown a woman's body, but I was still self-conscious about it, not proud. Even in hot weather, I wore sweaters to smother my breasts.

Lindy and Margie quickly paired up with the dark-haired boy and his best friend, who was blond and also seventeen. That left me with the oldest boy, a skinny, bepimpled nineteen-year-old who'd already started college. As leftovers, he and I exchanged almost no words and joined the others around the campfire, where they passed us a tin pot of spiked Kool-Aid. Before long, Lindy, Margie, and their "dates" disappeared into the woods.

My boy and I remained silent by the campfire for about ten minutes, and then he asked if I wanted to go sit under the tarp, twined to four trees a few feet away. I thought I knew what "sitting under the tarp" would mean: petting, where, I'd heard, you might take your blouse off, and I was not ready for it, especially with an older boy I didn't know, who would have accepted any girl supplied that night. Yet I went along with him, frightened that he might get angry if I didn't, afraid that if I let go of his hand and sought my own tent in the dark, I'd crash into my mother's cot. The sky was black, the moon the barest slice of light.

Any minute now this will all fall through, I thought. This boy won't try anything. The others will come back.

And they did, but not before the boy leaned over and mashed his mouth against mine, his tongue rocketing past my teeth. What was this? "Advanced" is the only way I could have put it. Or "dirty." Not romantic, as I'd dreamed my first kiss would be.

"Wait," I cried, sliding away from him. "I'm only eleven years old."

"Sure you are," the boy said, reaching for me. "Sure, baby. Come on."

"I really am—only eleven," I said, turning my shoulder. "Eleven. I'm sorry."

The boy pulled back and saw I was telling the truth. His face relaxed, even, I thought, gave off a sad kindness. "I'm going to get the others," he said.

Back in our tent, Lindy and Margie barely spoke to me past a terse reminder to keep our escapade a secret. But someone had seen us, and word got back to the adults. A few days after the campout, my mother picked me up from school and announced we were going to the troop leader's house for a special meeting. "What kind of meeting?" I asked. She wouldn't say.

Lindy, her mother, and Margie were waiting for us in the living room. Lindy had applied hot pink lipstick for the occasion, but Margie wisely wore her Candy Striper's uniform. My mother and I sat on a loveseat across from them. Lindy's mother asked us girls directly: had we sneaked out late and met the boys? Yes, we nodded. Then she delivered a stern lecture—not about sex, as no one talked about it, then—but about propriety, reputations, following orders. I stared at my shoes the whole time. I dared not protest, but I knew I didn't deserve the lecture as much as Lindy and Margie did.

My mother and I pulled out of the troop leader's driveway, not speaking. She knew how I clammed up at confrontation, even when I had a right to defend myself, and she knew why I'd gone along with the older girls. But I didn't realize that, then; I assumed she was mad at me, or worse: disappointed. It wasn't until much later that I realized her last words on the subject were closer to an affirmation than a punishment.

When she'd driven us out of the troop leader's neighborhood, she slowed the car and turned her clear blue eyes toward my suffering brown ones. "You've been wanting to quit the Girl Scouts," she said. "Well, it's OK with me if you do."

《 《 《

My rocky adjustment to Titusville continued, partly because I'd been pulled from my last year of a stable, homogenous elementary institution and thrust into an exponentially growing junior high, loaded with tight cliques bred of the anxiety transience creates. I wasn't the only one struggling. Many incoming kids tried and tried again to gain a social foothold in a deeply stratified community of natives who had lived in the area well before NASA, early comers, including senior scientists and engineers, and the rest of us, attached to families working at the Space Center, providing support services, or starting businesses. Along with other students, I was unnerved by the county's progressive academic tracking system, which landed me in a class of two dozen other smarty-pants who, before moving to Titusville, had been tops in their schools. Where before, most of us had experienced little or no competition, just eagerly accomplished our work, now we watched our backs, for the more aggressive among us would derail the others with misinformation, cloak ambition with feigned nonchalance, stall a girl in the hall so her pal could sprint to the next class and turn in her history project, similar to yours, first. Had I been told I would one day work in academia, and known what I know now, I would have accepted this as early orientation. But at eleven, I just walked around in perpetual shock, wondering why people were so mean. I envied my sister, innocently navigating Whispering Hills Elementary, safe from the confusion of jumped-up teenagers: girls strutting in Cover Girl makeup and must-have Villager shirtwaists, sweaty boys shoulder-punching each other in the cafeteria and belching. For her, there was no angst over undressing in front of others in PE, hoping desperately Miss McNutt would let you skip the communal shower because you were on your period, or the sneer of the high-salaried scientist's daughter who asked if you'd sewn that Bobbie Brooks knockoff yourself.

《 《 《

Southern girls and transplanted Northern girls inevitably befriended one another, and often their upbringings clashed or failed to come to terms. To me, it appeared the conflicts stemmed, on the southern side, from family matriarchs, for Southern girls' mothers tended to be suspicious of "Yankees." Although many of these mothers had moved with their families from other states, they felt comfortable in Titusville, defending what was left of "the old ways," warning their children of outsiders. A few of my friends and acquaintances were dominated by what I privately called the Southern Ladies, born of a way of life I'd come to understand somewhat, but could never penetrate.

My first Southern friend, and her mother, offered a back-handed introduction to the culture. Kathy was a flute player in my beginning band class. Her family had moved to Titus-ville from the southeast corner of Missouri bordering Arkansas. I admired her rapt attention in junior high band rehearsals, her refusal to kowtow to boys, her disdain for fashion. She wasn't a belle, her accent wasn't pronounced, and so, I thought, her background might be closer to mine. I needed a friend. Already I had suffered the North-South split in sixth grade science class, taught by a Mrs. Smiley, who called most often on girls who shared her drawl, doting on them like daughters, chatting with them familiarly before and after class. I suspected they all attended the same church; perhaps Mrs. Smiley had been a guest in their homes.

Kathy and I sat next to each other in a couple of classes, hung around in the band room together after school, played duets, fantasized about our brilliant music careers even as we struggled to play "Twinkle, Twinkle, Little Star" in tune. It seemed we were a team, inseparable, and for a time, I imitated her distinctive cursive handwriting; instead of downward loops on lowercase *G*s, *J*s, and *Y*s, I sent down straight lines with backward hooks at the tail.

But one day I hailed her in American History and she didn't smile, just stared sternly, like a teacher about to deliver a failure notice—which, after a long pause, came.

"Ann," Kathy said, with more resolve than regret, "I can't associate with you any more."

"What?" I said. The word "associate," distant and formal, pointed to parental command. My stomach sank. "Why?"

"Because my mother said so."

"Why?" I repeated. What had I done?

"Because you talked in the movie."

"Huh?"

"You talked in the movie. It's impolite."

"You mean, when I said—about the horses?"

"Yes. I can't be friends with you any more. Sorry."

Just then, the bell rang for the start of class and the teacher rose to the chalkboard. Kathy turned to her textbook, and I opened mine, but couldn't focus on the lesson. I kept thinking back to the previous Saturday, when Kathy and I had met at the Magnolia Theater with our mothers to watch *The Miracle of the White Stallions*, a Disney movie about the Lipizzaners in Vienna. We were excited about the movie, had anticipated it for weeks; finally, it had come to Titusville. And because we wanted our mothers to know each other, to solidify our friendship, we'd invited them.

The four of us met in the lobby, made introductions and small talk. I noticed Kathy's mother was less relaxed than mine. Although she behaved cordially, her eyes were unfriendly. As we searched for empty seats in the crowded theater, Kathy's mother hung back, so that my mother entered the row first, followed by me, then Kathy. The two mothers sat farthest apart.

From that moment, we all faced the screen straight on for two hours, except toward the middle of the film, when one sequence so moved me I bent toward Kathy and whispered, "Aren't they beautiful?" Kathy nodded, our mothers nodded, and we all continued to watch the movie. When it ended, we exchanged polite good-byes and departed, each daughter eager to learn what Mom thought of her best friend. But apparently, something had been settled on Kathy's side even before the credits rolled. I had been rude to whisper, Kathy informed me, and summarily dismissed.

Kathy and I never spoke again. She avoided my eyes in rehearsal, and our paths suddenly didn't cross in the halls. I was astonished, that three words could disqualify me so. I played that scene over and over, wondering at what precise point Kathy's mother determined I didn't make the grade. Much later, I understood the reaction to my whisper had been a cover for something else Kathy's mother didn't like. It could have been anything: my mother's northern speech, erect carriage, level demeanor. Or was it my earnest, buck-toothed smile, the way I shouldered and re-shouldered my pocketbook, or—why not the way the Magnolia's front doors stuck in the humidity, or the mushy popcorn, the flimsy movie ticket?

I would never know, but as the years passed and two more Southern mothers expressed reservations about me, I understood I possessed a threatening difference. The mother of a competitive classmate told her daughter—who triumphantly passed the comment on to me—that I was being raised with too much freedom. "Helen McCutchan lets Ann do whatever she wants. She's too lax. It's not right." Another mother, a genuine former debutante, told her daughter I would never amount to anything, because I wasn't "disciplined." "She blows in and out of here," the mother complained. "Does she ever study?"

What a disgrace I was, raised by a permissive Yankee mother. Had I known the first girl would never live more than thirty miles from her parents, or ever marry, and that the second would take ten years to finish a bachelor's degree, I might have chuckled, as I do now. But I did not know the future, or where each Southern Lady's fears originated, and I was not yet confident of my own way of moving in the world. It's unfortunate, that pain easily lodges in the delicate flesh of becoming, before a particular aspect of self is fully formed. I wonder if we circle back to youth at midlife, not to relive it, but to draw out the thorns that, despite maturation, were never fully absorbed.

III

Music is a universal language, it's said, and it's true, that when everyone faces the same direction, toward a conductor, and their utterances are neither clipped nor drawled, but honked and slurred, from where one moved or who's calling the shots at home means very little, neither does one's calculus average. The group unites in pure, uninflected sound, with the goal of—if not creating beauty right away—at least bleating in sync with a plastic baton. It's not surprising that, as a musically inclined newcomer to Parkway's ever-shifting cultural and academic spectrum, in which so many children had recently been "the new kid," I found refuge in band—a group, after all.

I'd wanted to be part of a band or orchestra since learning to read music on the tonette, a plastic flute-like instrument offered in elementary school. The language had come easily, once I could name and finger the individual notes lined within larger gestures familiar from hymn-singing at Calvin Christian. I took pleasure in small revelations, like the correspondence between first line F and the waffling pitch I produced by covering the tonette's lone underside tone-hole with my left thumb and blowing lightly into the mouthpiece.

It was easy to overblow the tonette, to send up an erratic mess of overtones that sounded the way a sheaf of paper looks when the wind scatters it. On thumb F, I began to learn the art of gentle, consistent breathing. Adding my left forefinger to the first hole on the upper side of the tonette got me first line E. Then another finger, and another, D, C, B, A, down to the lowest note on the tonette, another, deeper F, all fingers down, all holes covered.

On the tonette or any other wind instrument, all notes are, in a sense, vowels, rousing a trunk full of air and the kaleidoscopic effects on the wood or metal it sets to humming. Musical sounds are abstract, open as wide as *A* or *O* to use and interpretation—a good match and a comfort to the reserved person who nevertheless has a lot to express.

Given my first clarinet, it took me days to produce anything close to a clarinet tone. When I finally barked an open G, I jumped from the impact of the sound and the physical effort it took to play that one note. But soon I learned to breathe properly for the new instrument, to pull in a cubic foot of air in one thrilling swoop, and release it in a consistent, malleable stream through the clarinet's mouthpiece, causing the reed to vibrate smartly, like the wing of a hummingbird.

When you push air from the pulsing deep bin of your body into the waiting column of a cured wood instrument, a kind of grace may sweep up along with it, tending to the letting go. It is in this moment that a girl knows she must keep doing this thing, at whatever cost, that the making of music with the body is grace. It is the whoosh of life she has longed for, the open door, the wide horizon.

❲ ❲ ❲

My father's first Titusville office, in a ground unit of a small, two-floor building, close to downtown, was as rudimentary as the Central Avenue duplex: just functional, furnished with two secondhand desks and a few chairs. Yet Apollo Insurance and Mortgage was his, not a corporation's, and the day he affixed his new business sign to the outside wall, the four of us proudly gathered around it, Mom stepping aside to snap pictures. Dad ordered advertising giveaways like those he'd mailed out from Equitable: cardboard desk calendars embossed with the company address and phone number, paper sleeves for insurance policies. In twelve years of business, he ran Apollo himself, with the exception of a few months or a year here and there, when he could afford a part-time secretary. His location changed twice more, presumably for a better space or lower rent.

Dad, Estalene, and I could count on unchanging trajectories for the next few years: Apollo Insurance for him, school for us. But Mom continually improvised a working life, as Titusville, and Brevard County, had no need for a professional Girl Scout— at least not one from New England. Soon after we arrived, she took a correspondence course in speed writing, a dictation method, and rented a typewriter, practicing that old skill on the kitchen table. She took a secretarial job at the Titusville Chamber of Commerce, where within a year she established herself as an expert on all things local and was featured in the Titusville *Star-Advocate* under the headline, "She's a Quiz Queen, Mostly." In the picture, she is squatting in the front office in her old Girl Scout camping duds and a bandanna headband, brushing a fresh coat of paint on a tourist brochure rack and smiling good-naturedly as if to say: "Come on in, the water's fine!"

The next year, she took a course in professional writing at Brevard Junior College in Cocoa, fifteen miles south, with the hope of finding employment at the cape. For a research project, she investigated a dairy in south Florida that played classical music to its cows, claiming higher yields. The paper required a trip back to Fort Lauderdale—a chance to visit friends. Mom finished the course just as construction on the Vehicle Assembly Building began and was hired as secretary to the head construction engineer. She worked with him in a trailer on site, and became, by far, the family member who knew best what was going on out there.

My mother enjoyed that job, impressing us over dinner with descriptions of the VAB: one of the largest buildings in the world, with four bays to assemble Apollo and Saturn rockets;

so immense it could generate its own weather system. She, who would stand in awe of a nesting turtle, a diving cormorant, or another glorious sunset, grew fascinated by engineering feats, the way an immense rocket could be built on a giant platform, and the platform carried at a snail's pace to the launchpad on a crawler-transporter with continuous double tracks, modeled on those of an army tank. Each tread shoe, she told us, weighed a whole ton. At lunchtime, she left the trailer in her new high heels and Lady Manhattan shirtwaist and picked her way down to a nearby cove to feed hot dogs to alligators. She liked her boss, who, we gathered, was a terrible speller. The building site's stressful atmosphere led to extreme behavior, she told us. One day, without provocation, a man in her trailer climbed up on his desk, flapped his arms and squawked like a chicken. Another time, a crane operator hoisted and swung a portable toilet occupied by an ill-tempered nurse, drawing cheers from the construction crew.

But in 1966 the VAB was completed, and soon her job, like so many temporary assignments at the cape, ended. Our family attended a grand open house for employees' families, stood in the vast maw of a structure equal, in volume, to nearly four Empire State Buildings, and gaped. We were even rained upon, proof of the self-generating weather system. And then Mom was home again, refreshing her résumé. In her last position, she transcribed medical records at Jess Parrish Memorial Hospital, named for the founder of the Nevins Fruit Company, whose great citrus packing house loomed by the train tracks across the highway. Here, she sat all day in a windowless room wearing pantsuits and earphones, taking down doctors' reports.

In Fort Lauderdale, her announcements at dinner had thrilled us: "We found a new camp site in the Everglades!" or "Five thousand Girl Scouts in one stadium, lighting candles and singing!" From the VAB, she'd delivered daily news of scientific feats accomplished a short walk from her desk. Now we heard, "Did you know doctors mumble?" and "You should see the cute piggy banks on sale in the hospital gift shop." There was nothing at Jess Parrish to whet her enthusiasm. It was all indoors. She worked in a pod. No one knew who she was.

One Saturday, her boss at the hospital invited the two of us on a shopping trip to Orlando. The women rode in front; I took the back seat. My mother's boss was, like my mother, in her early fifties, but had not a fraction of my mother's poise and refinement. She was chunky, sloppily dressed, her hair a fixed pile of hay, while my mother was casually but flatteringly attired and coiffed. The boss chattered the full thirty two-lane miles to Orlando, as if my mother were her inferior and obligated to bear a monologue, and somewhere along that marshland route, my mother's boss regaled us with the tale of an opera career she'd given up for marriage—a happy martyr, she was. I didn't believe for a moment she'd had that career, but I decided right then that I would never make such a sacrifice, and I hurt for my silent mother, who had.

《 《 《

Because I practiced my clarinet every day, devotedly gumming "Sheep May Safely Graze" and "To a Wild Rose" in my bedroom, Mom went in search of a private teacher, finding but one choice in town: Mr. Kirk, proprietor of Kirk's School of Music, a brown, termite-ridden ranch house close to the top of Tropic Street, surrounded by cabbage palms. Mr. Kirk, whose credentials we never questioned, ushered me through the screened front door, and, stepping into his yeasty living room, I assumed its strange odor was just Old Man. I followed him eagerly to an enclosed porch, where I assembled my rented plastic instrument and sat primly on a folding chair, alert and ready for my life to change.

Mr. Kirk placed an empty music stand before me and took a seat at his desk, to my left. Against the porch windows, thick blades of tall iron plants, old as a previous homestead, clapped and shuddered in the wind. "Relax, honey," Mr. Kirk said, "Your lesson's a whole thirty minutes, and we'll have a good old time." How jolly he was, this smiley, bespectacled old man with his soft, sagging torso and the kind of white hair that turns yellow. I centered a new Rico reed against my mouthpiece facing, and twisted the ligature's screws, not too tight.

"Your mother says you're talented—first chair at Parkway!" said Mr. Kirk. "We'll start with this book. It'll cost $2.95, and you can pay me next time." From a file cabinet, he pulled out a red and yellow volume a half-inch thick titled *World's Greatest Music for Clarinet*. I took it from Mr. Kirk and opened to pages so black with notes I thought he had made a mistake. I wasn't this advanced.

But either he believed I was, or he didn't care whether the music was appropriate for me; it was what he had for sale. And I was flattered, too—maybe I *was* ready for those horizontal ladders of sixteenth notes, and only a teacher with Mr. Kirk's expertise could see it!

My first assignment was "Poupée Valsante," or "The Dancing Doll," a trifling Hungarian chestnut. Its sprightly, tricky rhythms required me to pat my foot firmly, beginning to end, to stay on track, especially after Mr. Kirk returned from the break he took in the middle of every lesson ("Excuse me, dear, I'm a bit thirsty"). Fondling a tall glass of golden, foaming liquid, he exhorted me to play "The Dancing Doll" faster, faster, *faster*, thumping his free hand on the desk in a tempo much faster than the reasonable one I'd set. By the end of the piece, I felt I'd been pushed off a cliff, and was dancing in air like the cabbage palms, their shaggy heads tossed in the swift hillcrest breezes, windmilling like deranged mops.

Worse, when Mr. Kirk ordered me to repeat "The Dancing Doll" (which was the way we filled the time—repetition, little instruction), he obliterated my efforts, singing along in his cracked old voice, hitting only the primary notes, ignoring the linking ornamentation and the time it took for me to jam it all in. He rushed me, he covered me up; yet for a time, his strange oppression goaded me. I wanted that much to learn, to master the instrument, to make real music—which, I suppose, separated me from those who'd follow this passion under the worst tutelage and those who'd understandably quit. At home I shoved my new mechanical metronome's weight ever lower on the inverted pendulum, forcing that doll well past a waltz. Soon, she danced like a dervish, jerky and shrill, and could outpace Mr. Kirk's thumps, his sorry blurts.

A few pieces later ("The Clarinet Polka," "Variations on Old, Black Joe") I'd grown sick of this game, and twice, Mr. Kirk had moved his arrhythmic hand from his desk to my knee. Both times, I adjusted my seating position to shake him off, and soon the school year ended. I never told my mother about it. When Mr. Kirk phoned her in September to schedule my lessons, I shook my head at her: No. "Then you tell him yourself," she said, handing me the phone. I don't know what I said to him— probably something about too many band rehearsals. He yelled at me, drunk, and I hung up on him.

The next year, Mom located a young Florida State clarinet graduate in Orlando and drove me over six times for lessons, paid for by Grandmother and Grandfather Bond, who now wintered in Titusville, in an apartment complex a block from us. The new teacher assigned me an arrangement of a Bee-

thoven piano sonata adagio to introduce me to a masterpiece, and to slow me down. It was a good choice, and it pleased my new piano accompanist, my mother, for she had recently purchased an upright piano, resurrecting a talent we hadn't known about. She had, she revealed, studied piano for years in Bangor, played with her high school orchestra and accompanied a local marimba soloist. At Streep's Music showroom in Orlando, she researched uprights carefully, playing memorized scraps of Percy Grainger's "Country Gardens" on each model and pinging individual keys repeatedly, asking my sister and me what we thought of the tone. We agreed the new brand, Yamaha, had the sweetest sound for the money she had set aside.

The Beethoven arrangement was a revelation: harmonically complex, with a melancholy melody and wandering, searching ornamentation, to be executed rubato, the antithesis of the cartoonish doll. But one can't deliver a convincing improvisatory effect, much less negotiate Beethoven's emotional twists and turns, without first possessing an even technique, which, thanks to my breakneck fling with "The Doll," I did not have. When I performed the Beethoven in a contest with my mother tracking me carefully on the piano, the wise judge wrote: "This piece requires a maturity well beyond your years."

IV

After a year on Central Avenue, Dad purchased a house in a new development off Garden Street, the state road ambling toward the "World's Longest Free Fishing Pier." The pier, once part of a wooden bridge edged out by a cement causeway shooting to NASA's north entrance, attracted locals equipped with rods, reels, and ice chests, and at night, shrimp nets, and was adjacent to the town's marina.

Our tiny neighborhood, lamentably named White Acres, contained twenty-five homes on a loop and cross street, squeezed in between the Garden Park Apartments and Oaklawn Memorial Gardens, the town cemetery. Our place, No. 21 Lynwood Avenue, had three bedrooms and one-and-a-half baths, totaling 1,050 square feet. Dad paid $13,500 for it.

White Acres lay just south of the Central Avenue duplexes, the two connected by an unpaved dogleg. As once I'd claimed a thicket adjacent to Bel-Air for private musings, I took that sandy trail as a refuge, for a time. Yet I didn't dawdle there, following the slow revolutions of light against morning glories, measuring breezes by the turns and spinnings of leaves; instead, I walked back and forth between Central and the asphalt tongue at the edge of the new development, somewhat intently, like a monk on a non-errand, and later rode my bike—it was the quickest way from White Acres to the public library. After I got my driver's license (on the second try; the first time, I knocked down some cones), I drove back there, faster and faster, until the dog-leg was no longer a shred of pastoral dream but a hallucina-tion, with thick, trick roots and looming sand humps that spun the tires to skidding, or swallowed them, depending on how recently it had rained.

I liked taking chances on the dogleg rather than riding primly out of White Acres to Garden Street, and continued to tear up the link in Dad's Ford Falcon until one dark night, after a hard storm, when the cicadas roared in the trees, and I joined the melee, popping the stick in neutral and sliding joyfully down the steepest, muddiest part, fishtailing to a stop before a wide puddle. There, caught in the headlights, stood a small owl at the puddle's center. I had never seen an owl on the ground; I thought they stayed in trees and hooted all night, flying only to catch a meal. Surely this owl would realize its mistake here, and move. But it did not. Its head swiveled toward my windshield, eyes blazing. I had no choice but to back up the hill and take the paved road home.

The experience—the shock of that owl, the power of one glaring bird—led me on an unsystematic mission to trace more of Titusville's back roads by car, for who knew what I would encounter? I'd heard rumors of a dead girl in a glass-front casket propped up to face the Indian River, but never could find her. Neither could I find "the haunted house" later revealed to be the run-down homestead of an old Titusville family—I'd actu-ally been to a party there. But after one hurricane or tropical storm—Gladys, Isbell, Abby?—I took the Indian River Road on a good hunch and stopped to walk by the swollen waterway and disheveled bank. Clouds lay so thick across the water the Vehicle Assembly Building, normally as prominent as the Washington Monument, was blotted out, gone. It seemed I stood in ancient weather, perhaps in a wrecked Indian village, among beached rafts, frond lean-tos, smoking fires. Inside a long thrust of wind, fanning palms clacked, hinged oaks moaned, while at water's edge, waves ticked and smacked against rocks and refuse. Little frogs sang. I stepped off the road and plunged into the mess of dizzy, fallen tropicals, was grabbing at dislocated limbs for balance when I heard a cry—a high, skinny sound propelled by breath, not friction—and stepped high through the blow-down to meet it, down by the river's lip. The cry seemed to have arisen from beneath, as if trapped, so I paused and waited until it arose again, closer, from a pile of bracken, rounded, like an overturned basket. I leaned across part of a wild orange to view the pile, and from the humped twigs a yellow beak shot up, opened, and declared itself.

The bird allowed me to part the branches and scoop him up, his beak quivering. He was large and mostly pink, appearing to have been plucked of black feathers, with a few stragglers sticking out, and so, I thought, he was damaged, though later I gathered he was undergoing his first molt. I climbed back to the road and drove home, the bird in my lap. I made a box nest in the utility room, fed him from an eyedropper, and very quickly, his feathers started to grow in. His skinny cry roughened to a bracing caw. "That's a crow," Dad said. I named him Edgar.

Although Edgar was large, he had not learned to fly, so he walked everywhere: from the box to my hand, to my arm, to a porch chair, to the ground, if I bent down. It seemed unnatural: a crow strutting across the Saint Augustine, pecking at vittles between the blades, deftly avoiding our resident armadillo's unreliable path, returning and climbing to my open palm.

One day, I decided I should encourage him to lift off. I stuck my arm in his box and he hopped right on for the trip to the backyard. I stood us in the center, in full sun. "OK, Edgar," I

said. "You'll know how to do this." I raised my bird arm and
flapped it, forcing the crow to spread his wings for balance. Still,
he clung, his talons gripping my flesh in confusion. Over and
over I flapped, until at last he let go, levitated for an instant,
and, with a surprised caw, made sloppy flight for the nearest
tree.

Edgar looked back at me—a little betrayed, but utterly
belonging to his first branch. And so he became a yard bird,
staying strictly within the confines of our lot. You had only to
call his name and he would drop down from a ficus, orange,
or oak, and perch on your shoulder. If you were a man with a
foil cigarette pack in your breast pocket, you'd risk losing the
shiny paper, because Edgar would gun for it, peck it up, maybe
tear your shirt. It became a family game. Would he go for
silver-toned sunglasses? A fork? An aluminum pie plate? To all,
yes.

Word of Edgar spread throughout the neighborhood: The
McCutchans have a trained crow—it stays in their backyard
and comes when called! One day, I came home from school
and called to Edgar, as usual. Nothing happened. I inspected
the yard's perimeter, past the screened porch, the septic tank,
the clothesline, the cement wall separating us from the Garden Park Apartments, calling and calling his name. Nothing
replied; I heard only the grainy traffic on Garden Street, the
grunts of a lawn mower several houses down. Maybe Edgar had
decided to fly away. Maybe he had died. I didn't believe either.
We talked to close neighbors. No clues. A few weeks later, someone two blocks over said he thought he'd seen "that retarded kid
from the next development" come by—couldn't be sure when,
exactly—tugging a red wagon with "what looked to be" a homemade birdcage.

❪ ❪ ❪

We had been in the new house just a few weeks when President Kennedy was assassinated in Dallas. November 22 was a Friday; Parkway students had just finished lunch and, eager for a weekend of surfing or sunbathing to begin, had tramped to History or English or Math or in my case, Band. I was sharing the first clarinet stand with Gerald, a bad boy who propped Ian Fleming novels in front of our part to "Stars and Stripes Forever" and opened them to the sex scenes.

Just as Mr. Keaton had once used the intercom for "Duck and Cover," Parkway's principal, Mr. Robertson, broke in with that bald, horrifying announcement: the president had been shot. The band room went silent, as if a foot of snow had dropped from the ceiling. Everyone, from the flutists, front row on the floor, all the way up to the percussion and tubas atop the highest riser, stared at the intercom, not breathing, anticipating a longer story, or even a retraction. Mr. Lewis, the band director, held up a hand—the habit of the junior high teacher on guard for an outburst.

Or was it a move toward comfort? A few seconds passed. The intercom crackled again, and we heard Mr. Robertson clear his throat. "Everyone may go home now," he said, his voice trembling. "School is canceled the rest of the day." One by one, we began to whisper among ourselves, and to weep.

Because President Kennedy had been chief champion of the space program, everyone in Titusville wondered if it, too, would be felled. At home, families anxiously discussed the possibility. Was the next move coming sooner than expected? If big contracts with Boeing or McDonnell Douglas or Chrysler were canceled, would their engineers be offered projects elsewhere? What about those in the recent influx of support services? Should the family with the cleaning contract at Mission Control return to Illinois and start over? Should the studio artist installing exhibits in NASA's visitor's center apply for graduate study? What about the school system? The area had attracted the best and brightest young teachers, with more coming. Would the open-air porticoes empty out and the virtual neighborhood of portable classrooms be hauled away? With a mass exodus, how would anyone unload a house, and, for those who stayed, what would be left of the town?

There was little discussion at our dinner table; my parents waited quietly, characteristically shielding my sister and me with silence, or references to others' situations, not theirs. At nearly fifty-seven, my formerly peripatetic father may not have predicted, much less wanted, another job-related move. My mother, philosophical and practical about change, might have imagined what her husband could face, how to help him, and how to retool her skills again.

Yet everyone's fears were short-lived; Kennedy's death didn't dismantle the space program—it galvanized it. As former NASA flight director Gene Kranz said, "it moved from being a challenge to literally a crusade. This was now our mission to win this battle, for President Kennedy. It was visceral, it was gut, we are going to do it, and we're the right people to do it, and we're going to do it in the time frame he said we'll do it."

NASA would make good on that vow, to land a man on the moon by the end of the decade, one month after my class graduated Titusville High School. James Ansell, one of my classmates, recalled deadlines forcing his father to stay at the cape for days. Eventually, his dad and three colleagues "would show up at the house at 2:00 a.m. and Mom would make them all breakfast. Dad would break out the bourbon and they sat around the kitchen table and talked about their projects in a proud, reflective mode. I was in awe at how smart they were, how they overcame massive obstacles as a team."

The pressure was on throughout the space community, to accomplish the extraordinary within the next six years, and we teenagers literally tracked Apollo's urgency toward our own adulthood—as if we, too, would ride a *Saturn V* to the moon. Kranz was right: it was visceral, it was gut, down to the youngest of us. In my life, no other campaign so permeated shared youth, so flavored the air we breathed.

☾ ☾ ☾

Titusville's position on the Indian River, famous for Florida's sweetest oranges, had once attracted large citrus packinghouses, which, in season, operated full tilt, supplying trucks and railroad cars bound across the country. But by the 1960s, the state's citrus production had begun to decline, as more and more land was bought up for residential and commercial development. Some developers saved a few orange trees from the backhoe; we had two in our yard, and the single vacant lot in White Acres, between our house and another, represented the original wild state, having an orange, clumps of palmetto—one tall enough to sport spiky old leaf bases, or "bootjacks"—a few pines, and poison ivy. In an urban echo to her Everglades breakout, Mom suffered a full-body onslaught from that piece of ground. On a windy day, gusts carried essence of ivy to damp bedsheets on our clothesline, and that night, swathed in sun-dried cotton, she itched, neck to toes. "The vacant lot attacked you!" we joked.

To soothe her irritated skin, Mom headed for salt water: the beach. But it wasn't a simple trip, as it had been in Fort Lauderdale. To get to the ocean from Titusville, one took the causeway over the river to Merritt Island, drove past the north entrance to

the Space Center, and continued on an old asphalt road winding through marsh to Playalinda Beach. You couldn't be there "in a few," like people in Cocoa or Melbourne, and you had to bring everything with you, since the beach, now under the government's auspices, had few amenities; forgetting a critical towel or six-pack meant driving all the way back to the mainland, or at least to the one beer and bait shop along the way that hadn't shut down yet. As well, Playalinda was frequently closed for mission preparations and launches, including unmanned operations that didn't make the news. Using Playalinda meant keeping a close eye on NASA's schedule. The launchpads were in plain view, just down to the right of your beach umbrella.

But what an exceptional beach it was—the finest, wildest beach in Brevard County, arguably of Florida's Atlantic coast, protected simply because it protected the Space Center. Had I been inclined to surf, I would have gone out every weekend, as the surfer kids did, loading their boards atop station wagons, in pickup trucks, and the back seats of convertibles, zooming across the causeway, sun-bleached hair flying behind them. There was some cachet to dating a fellow who surfed; I once overheard a girl in gym class brag about her new boyfriend, thus: "He may not be that cute—but he has a *board*."

I had no board, knew no one who had one, and drove out to Playalinda only occasionally with friends or my parents, not for lack of surfing expertise (for only a small number were very good at it), but because I felt self-conscious in a bathing suit. My favorite pastimes at Playalinda were bouncing far out in the surf or lying face down on my towel. With my nose in salty terry cloth and a transistor radio clapped to one ear, I listened alternately to Marvin Gaye and the waves lifting, then falling on the shore. Every twenty minutes my trance was interrupted by the radio station's perky reminder: "Time to turn, so you won't burn." I pulled in my tummy, rolled to my back, and submitted my front to the warming sun, heavy on my kneecaps, ribs, eyelids.

But there were times when I tossed the radio aside and sat up straight on my towel, or left it to dig a shallow nest in the sand, settling in, leaning back on my elbows and forearms, watching the sea glide forward, fatten and stretch up into a curl, brimming with white ruffles. At that moment, that breathless upbeat, a wave seemed complete as a painting, as if it contained all the motion to follow.

And then the curl dropped to its inevitable tumble, collapsing into the smooth glass left by its predecessor.

And as the wave dissolved, and the glass slid back into the current, my gaze lifted far beyond, to a straight line separating marine blue from azure, promising indefinable depth and loft, infinite, both of which I wanted. Always, I would need this endless view, and not because I sought its secret terminus, a riddle solved, but because I knew it had neither of these, and I was a very small thing looking out at the unknown, and found comfort in that.

☾ ☾ ☾

Soon after we moved to White Acres, I took an interest in baking. There is no explanation for it, though it might have come from the impulse to make something, anything. Mom was no baker; she made only one cake in those years: a recipe someone pressed on her involving Duncan Hines white cake mix, a can of fruit cocktail, and a packet of coconut flakes. It was too sweet; she never repeated it and we never asked for it. But I was drawn to the idea of preparing and mixing ingredients just so and producing a delicious cake, loaf, or plate of cookies, and Mom was willing to get me started, offering her single resource:

the American Woman's Cookbook, 1943 Victory edition, green, thick and blocky as a Bible, and dedicated "with affection and gratitude" to General Douglas MacArthur. Facing the dedication page was a stern portrait sketch of the hero in uniform, an American flag rippling behind him.

"His heroic leadership and gallant fight against overwhelming odds should inspire every American woman to make the most of daily opportunities to support the war effort in her home and in every sphere of worthwhile war activity," the inscription read. "There must be thousands of little ways to do a job better— thousands of opportunities to help—to create, conserve, and to serve. If every woman, every day, in everything she does, will do her utmost to accomplish the aims of our Government, then that combined effort will soon become a gigantic and valuable aid toward winning the war."

The book included a special chapter on wartime cookery, which stressed soups, meatless dishes, canning produce harvested from a Victory garden, and saving cooking fat for reclamation—not for food, but for "the manufacture of munitions and soap."

1943: it must have been a wedding gift. But how grim, this trumpet call to patriotism, to be enacted even over the soup kettle or cooling rack.

Flipping past General MacArthur, I discovered a recipe for Foundation Cake and set to work in a cloud of pure white Gold Medal flour, sifting the dry ingredients, creaming the butter and sugar, beating the eggs with joy. In a little more than an hour, I removed my cake from our Harvest Gold GE oven, frosting it with Eggless Confectioners' Frosting, a lifeless but serviceable mixture of sugar, milk and vanilla.

I made that cake over and over, adding nuts or orange juice for extra flavor, moving on to Chocolate Nut Cake and Pineapple Cake, and most of the cookies, molasses and fudge squares being my favorites. By the time I was required to take Home Economics in the eighth grade, I was confident of my baking skills, despite setting the kitchen on fire in a deep-fat doughnut experiment (Dad's stout insurance policy covered paint and new roosters-at-sunrise wallpaper). I began inventing my own desserts, ignoring the teacher's interminable cautions about following instructions for basic sugar cookies. "I don't even need a recipe," I told Mrs. McCauley, who gave me a B for smugness.

So with high confidence one December I determined to make a Christmas fruitcake, and my mother, clueless about what that would take, but willing, as always, to see me try something new under her auspices, took me to buy the ingredients. From the recipe in the wartime cookbook we made a list and trolled the aisles of the Titusville A&P, searching for one pound of citron, two pounds of raisins, three pounds of currants. It never occurred to either of us that materials given in pounds, not cups, indicated a monstrous yield.

The dry ingredients alone filled our medium bowl, so I shook them into the large one. Adding the currants brought the mix to the edge of it, and there were still seven additions to go, including nine eggs. I searched the utility room for a larger container, and among mildewed back issues of *Reader's Digest*, Dad's tarnished Equitable Life sales trophies, and various small animal cages, I found a large white enamel pail Mom had used for camping. You could carry water or kindling in it. You could pee in it, too.

I lugged the thing into the kitchen and continued mixing the fruitcake. I couldn't add the final ingredient—one cup of strong coffee—without risking a spill, so I carefully lifted the pail off the counter and set it on newspapers I'd spread along the floor. In went a cup of Folgers instant, and the wooden spoon to stir it. The batter rose and eased down the pail sides.

My mother remarked on the great quantity. "You'll have to use all the cake pans, the loaf pans, and the metal bowls," she said, and helped me gather everything. There were so many cakes I baked some in saucepans. It took four shifts; I was up all night.

The fruitcake, though delicious, became the bane of the neighborhood. This was high season for local pecans and citrus, and everyone else was making pralines, sour orange pie, and lemon squares, not pushing figgy pudding's heavy-set cousin on innocent victims. There was so much cake I couldn't remember who I'd given it to until an offer was met with "No thanks" and a quick turn of the heel. The postman accepted two packages; a good sign, I thought, from the man who knew our household had a double subscription to the Frederick's of Hollywood lingerie catalog. But that is another story.

Where's the Moon?

I

Loren Eiseley wrote of "a silence as dreadful as that of the moon," which describes the kind of quiet I discovered in the cemetery abutting White Acres. Although Oaklawn fronted on Garden Street, its oldest plots lay in the very back, slightly northwest of White Acres, and one day I struck out past the last house in the subdivision, through moss-hung trees and scrub, to a line of lichened gravestones that had been wedged in the earth decades earlier. One marked an infant's brief life with a rough sculpture of a lamb. It brought to mind Haverill, the mysterious predecessor Mom had recently described to me: "Her hair was auburn; we don't know where that came from." It was here, where the grass grew taller, the trees thicker, that I began to wonder about my parents' pasts, for I had begun keeping a daily diary more capacious than the lock-and-key variety, and the sense that I was accumulating a personal history pointed to theirs. Until now, they had been monolithic, lacking complexity, for after all, they were my parents, and good ones. Now, in the oldest corner of the cemetery, I tried to imagine what they had been like as children, who, like I, had played with toys, learned manners, attended school. Such brooding could create silence close to that Eiseley described—a deafness, an insularity —despite the intermittent tire drone from Garden Street, the ratchet and burr of an engine at the nearby airfield. But in time, the quiet sank even deeper, and that oblivious stratum came alive with subtle sounds: breezes humming within the oaks and magnolias, playing leaf fans like harmonicas, bamboo like rhythm sticks. The clicking of pine needles. The ebb and flow of it all suggested song and intimate conversation; it is true: you can hear grass whisper. Often, meditations in this orphan patch set between starter homes and fresh-dug crypts evoked a Bach chorale from band rehearsal a few hours before. Lodged in my ear, the hymn seemed to break forth anew in the woods' windy resonance, a phantom choir in four-part harmony.

《　《　《

It was small, just inside the front door, easy to miss. We each stored one coat for the mild Florida winters in that closet, though I can't see any of them now. What I do notice are two artifacts from their earlier lives. For Mom, a full-length black velvet opera cape with reinforced shoulders, satin lining, and a bold faux-amethyst closure. To go with it, mother-of-pearl opera glasses secreted in her jewelry box. But never in my lifetime did she wear or use these items, unless in Washington, when I was very young. Throughout my teens, the spectacular opera cape hung in a sleek column alongside salt-rotted windbreakers and off-kilter sweaters, like a dignified old diva who stands her ground among riffraff, hoping for a comeback.

For Dad, it is a small five-ringed notebook stored high on the hat shelf, containing original poems in his hand, penciled, barely legible. (I've often wondered if he was a lefty, forced to train right.) At least one was a military rouser with a refrain like, "So on we boys, and on we boys, and on with guns we're marching." The poems cleaved to sturdy meters and rhymed, like those by poets he might have learned in school: the Hoosier James Whitcomb Riley (*Little Orphant Annie*, *The Raggedy Man*) who used central Indiana dialect, and the Illinois poet Vachel Lindsay (*General William Booth Enters into Heaven*). Both poets toured widely, declaiming their work to enthralled audiences;

Lindsay, especially, was nothing less than a performance art-ist. Perhaps it was in the tradition of the public lyceum that my father recited poetry as a young man at Yellowstone Park and felt moved to write his own. The notebook is long gone, but the knowledge of it is a talisman, a possible but undefined link to my father's inner life.

☾ ☾ ☾

As an adult I've moved fairly often, and each time, objects I've forgotten have come closer to light, either because I suddenly noticed them in the packing process or rearranged them in the new residence. My parents' books, in Fort Lauderdale tucked away in a spare bedroom, were now shelved in a pair of brown bookcases Mom bought to stand along the dining nook wall between the door to the carport and the ironing closet. Most of the books harked back to postwar days, as if my parents had stopped reading around 1955. Some bore a Book of the Month Club designation. Here are some titles:

We Took to the Woods, by Louise Dickinson Rich, 1942. A plainspoken chronicle of a couple that follows a dream, living and raising a family in Maine's backwoods.

Rachel Carson's *The Sea Around Us*, first edition, 1951. The environmentalist Rachel Carson lived near us in suburban Maryland and in 1953 moved to Maine.

Witness, the 1952 autobiography of Whittaker Chambers, the communist spy who testified in the perjury and espionage trial of his former friend and comrade, Alger Hiss. Hiss was con-victed of perjury in "the trial of the century" and served time in prison; Chambers, who had previously lied under oath, was, as a government witness, immune. The book galvanized Eisenhower conservatives like my parents.

From Then 'Til Now: A History of the Village Called

McCutchanville, by Kenneth P. McCutchan, 1955. First produced in a limited printing, it was issued again by the Indiana Historical Society in 1969. Among other things, this book explains how a fight between two brothers resulted in the tiny community's pair of Methodist churches, about a mile apart. To discover which of the two McCutchan-stuffed cemeteries contains your relations, you have to know which brother you descended from.

The Methodist *Book of Discipline*. A slender paperback, black and yellow. This may have been the single unread book on the shelf, its binding was so tight. It may have been a gift for joining Titusville First Methodist.

The Upper Room. Not a book, but issues of a Methodist daily worship guide Mom subscribed to for a short time, in an effort to unite the family for dinner. We were all just too independent, going every which way, she observed, with a light note of despair, and suggested we read aloud from *The Upper Room* every night around the table. For each day of the month, there was a Bible verse, a short lesson, and a prayer, and we intoned these for a time, taking turns, extending our thanksgiving beyond the traditional grace Dad had mumbled for years ("Mumblemumblemumble . . . and us to thy service, Amen"). But the practice didn't hold. Someone had to work late. Someone was invited to dinner at a friend's house. Someone had band practice.

Tales of the South Pacific, by James Michener, Reader's Digest Condensed Version. *South Pacific*, about wartime love and intrigue, won the Pulitzer Prize for fiction in 1948. We also had the LP soundtrack to the 1958 Rodgers and Hammerstein musical with Mitzi Gaynor and Rossano Brazzi. My favorite songs were "Some Enchanted Evening" and "I'm Gonna Wash That Man Right Outa My Hair."

A boxed set of Shakespeare's plays—two volumes of comedy, two of tragedy. Green bindings. Near-pristine condition. The type is too small even for the sharpest of eyes, yet my sister still lugs them with her every time she moves. They're currently jammed on a closet shelf over her hiking gear, in western Colorado.

Winnie the Pooh and *When We Were Very Young*, by A. A. Milne. 1950 editions. Given to me as a small child, and shared with Estalene when she was old enough. Mom and Dad read them aloud to us so often a few of the poems from the second book still ring in my head and limbs. You could dance to "The King's Breakfast," for instance.

The King asked
The Queen, and
The Queen asked
The Dairymaid:
"Could we have some butter for
The Royal slice of bread?"

World Book Encyclopedia, 1960 edition, bought when my sister and I were in the second and fourth grades. It informed many writing assignments. Some school reports sounded similar to a World Book entry.

How to Win Friends and Influence People, by Dale Carnegie. 1940s Pocket Book edition. The businessman's classic.

Baby and Child Care, by Dr. Benjamin Spock. The popular child-rearing guide, first published in 1946, encouraged parents to treat their children as individuals, not offspring. For decades, its prodigious sales stood second only to the Bible's.

The Holy Bible. King James Version. A small, black softcover, torn at the edges. Ant track print. It was inscribed to my mother, from her parents.

After Mom died, I inherited another Bible from her grandmother's family, a heavy 1850s volume with large print, etched Bible scenes, and center pages for entering births, marriages, and deaths. I found just enough space there to add my birth and my sister's and our parents' final dates, finishing out those pages. As if the Marden family Bible would dictate our line's closure, neither my sister nor I have borne children, and I imagine the tome will someday go to a historical society in Maine, where no one will know it lay for years in a central Florida closet, packed in a pink canvas beach bag behind an ironing basket and two roach traps.

Grimm's Fairytales, Andersen's Fairytales, two-volume set; Grosset & Dunlap, 1945. The tale I remember best is Andersen's "The Girl Who Trod on a Loaf"—because I loved the antique word "trod," the way you had to drop your jaw for that "ah" vowel and pull it up for the abrupt consonant "deh." And because the story had a creepy, moralistic ending, not the usual happy one. In it, the girl, a vain, nasty wench, tosses a fresh loaf of bread, a gift for her parents, into a puddle for a stepping stone, to avoid soiling her fine shoes. Down she sinks to the muddy realm of the evil Marsh Woman, a tortured hell from which no one ever returns.

How to Make Your Daydreams Come True, by Elmer Wheeler, published in 1952 by Prentice Hall, and still in print today. Our copy had a purple binding, and because Prentice Hall was spelled out in white at the base of its spine, I thought a man named Prentice Hall wrote it. It glowed from the new shelf like an oracle. I read it and tried to follow one part of its Master Formula, which was to write your dream on a piece of paper and tape it to the bathroom mirror so you'd see it first thing in the

morning and right before you went to bed. Thus were deeply
felt wishes and oral hygiene combined. The fantasy I posted on
the mirror? Oh, something to do with attracting boys or losing
weight.

❬ ❬ ❬

I don't claim these books represent my family's collective mind,
or an unchanging one, just as the presence of the original 1977
Moosewood Cookbook in my kitchen doesn't mean I still cook
with lots of cheese and sour cream (it doesn't even mean I cook).
But they were always there, shelved against the wall, as necessary to home as pots and pans, and none were for show, and all,
except possibly the Methodist *Book of Discipline*, had been read.

One book never made it to the shelves: Mary McCarthy's
1963 novel *The Group*, a paperback I found one day when I was
home alone, taking the opportunity to rifle through my mother's lingerie drawer. There it was, beneath a tousle of slips and
nightgowns, this book she thought to hide. The discovery was
only a little less than overwhelming; my mother was both a clear
spring and silent bedrock; *The Group*, I gathered, had surfaced
from a stratum in between.

Anyone might come home at any moment, so I opened to
a page at random, which happened to contain the only steamy
sex scene in the entire novel. But I didn't know that then. Based
on scant evidence that day, I thought Mom was reading a dirty
exposé about Vassar graduates doing it all over New York City.
My mother! Who so quietly acknowledged my first period, and
who, before that, had demanded I get rid of issues of *True Confessions* hidden in my stack of Betty and Veronica comic books.
My mother, gatekeeper of decency, a Girl Scout for God's sake.

If I'd been more curious, or less shocked, I would have
sneaked back regularly, read the whole novel, and come to a dif-

ferent understanding. But perhaps I'd gotten what I needed then: a hint, even a dissonant one, that my mother was interested in sex. When, long after her death, I finally read the novel beginning to end, her interest in *The Group* made more sense. Indeed, the heroines, well-educated young women of the 1930s beginning adult lives as professionals, wives and mothers, were her peers, and her past opened to me a little more, as did my own. For to some degree I identified with the central figure, Kay, the artistic one married to a charismatic theater man who lies and cheats on her, and tells her she has no talent, while she maintains responsibility for the marriage. Kay is the one who dies, of course—her funeral opens the book; hers is the death of a female's promise, of full potential—and her tale could have been a cautionary one for me, had *The Group* been shelved openly with the others.

《 《 《

Writers commonly claim they read early and voraciously; I did both, and received neither extraordinary praise nor derision for my habits. I preferred novels and biographies partly because they rendered lives, real or imagined, complete and whole. (I remember best biographies of brave, accomplished women, like Marie Curie, Jane Addams, Annie Oakley.) In fiction or nonfiction stories, questions raised were resolved in some inevitable, satisfying fashion, however complicated the work's development, like a symphony drifting or plunging toward its final chord. And I loved the sound of language, the orality of it, chewing on it, listening to it in my own silence. I haunted the library, as they say, fretted over the town's lack of a bookstore, read under the covers at night with a flashlight.

My relationship to book acquisition, though, suffered a setback our second year in Titusville, when the public library, another cinder-block special, called, asking for my overdue book, the one I was already checking out over and over again: *Your Future in Music.* Dad happened to be home to answer the phone, snapped at the request, put me in the car, drove me to the library, and marched me inside, announcing to the librarian in a low, firm voice that his daughter was not yet responsible enough for a library card, and it should be taken away from me. The librarian looked at us—he the angry parent, me the mortified teenager—and, granting me an apologetic expression, honored my father's wishes. I turned in the book, paid the twenty-five-cent fine, and handed over my card.

But why this, and not some other infraction? I had plenty of annoying habits: I talked on the phone constantly with my bandmates, kept a messy bedroom, scooped out all the chocolate from the Neapolitan ice milk with my index finger when no one was looking. The late book was worse, I understood later—I had failed a public contract, and so, apparently, I deserved a public humiliation. Dad's domain, as father, was public, and because he stepped in so seldom, his involvement made a deep impression on me. I understand that he overreacted for some reason having nothing to do with my tardy book, that the punishment did not fit the crime. Perhaps, as a new business owner in a small town, he wanted his family to appear highly responsible, of sterling character, and my carelessness, possibly noted by a gossipy librarian, might undermine it. Or he may have been suffering the generalized anxiety inherent in adjusting to a new life. I'll never know. But I confess that to this day, I am library-averse, preferring to buy rather than borrow, for almost as soon as I relax into a library book, I tell myself I must *plan ahead* to return the volume or risk receiving a note from the circulation desk, a stinging reprimand for my lax behavior. It was only in my forties, when I received a professor's privilege to keep library books for an entire semester, that I began, tentatively, to check them out of the university stacks, keeping them as long as I wanted, renewing them privately by typing my ID and clicking a mouse. And still, still, I am often late, apologizing to the student assistant behind the counter, as a parental figure who knows she has set a bad example and will be judged by the young.

II

In Titusville, the Equitable mailing jobs stopped. The ironing continued for a year or two, with a slight raise, until my sister and I abandoned it and Mom and Dad hired someone to do it. In time, they couldn't afford help, and it was every man for himself. Even Dad did his own shirts, until Mom bought him some no-iron poly-cottons on sale in Orlando. Once, I tried ironing one, and even though I set the heat on low, a chemical stink arose from the warmed sleeves, confirming my distaste for synthetic fabrics. Polyester leisure suits were years away; aesthetically, I was ahead of my time.

With no weeds to pull or envelopes to stuff, I was, the summer I turned thirteen, obliged to work outside my parents' orbit to earn money for items like a Beatles album or the bonnet hairdryer I coveted in the Sears catalog. Occasionally I babysat for young families down the block. My first clients were a junior high football coach and his wife, who had a toddler and infant. There was not much to do but help put the baby down and read the little girl a story, and after both had fallen asleep, I always headed into the pantry for the family's box of Nestlé's Quik, a powdered chocolate drink mix Mom and Dad wouldn't buy, and which, leaning against the doorjamb, I gobbled dry with a soup spoon. Another neighborhood couple, she a nurse, he a NASA engineer, both soft-spoken, with a tiny baby, engaged me several times when they went out to dinner. The baby was a hard sleeper; I never even picked it up. Instead, I spent the evenings listening to the couple's long-play records, all romantically inclined ("Blueberry Hill," "Moon River"), imagining Mr. and Mrs. on their first date, he in a suit and tie, she in a starched nurse's uniform. Would anything so sweet and proper ever happen to me? But one night I peeked in the marital bedroom and discovered on the wall a Sex Mood-Meter, a wooden clock with two hands (red for the woman, blue for the man), its twelve segments ranging from "If I'm not back in 10 minutes, start without me," to "NO!" This particular evening, the "girl" arrow was pointed to "Now, about that mink!" a winking flirtation, and I suddenly saw the quiet nurse as a tease, a sex bomb, pretending to decency in a concrete house with Formica countertops. When the couple returned, I stared at them, goony-eyed, trying to connect their fresh looks and placidity to the shameless, exciting mood meter. As they handed me my earnings with whispered thanks, I wondered: could they tell I knew all about their secret life?

One June, after school was out, a friend's mother offered me telephone survey work for *Today*, the new, county-wide Gannett paper that had eclipsed Titusville's *Star-Advocate*, the local rag Dad dubbed the Star-Aggravate. The *Star-Advocate* was unequivocally provincial; a supermarket opening might receive the same number of column inches as a racial incident at a football game, suggesting the reason some former residents still insist school integration was smooth. To be fair, the *S-A*'s Space Center updates were important and contained the most detailed writing in the paper, but the daily foci were national headlines pulled off the wire and urgent dispatches from the Little League and the Garden Club.

Not that my short-term assignment for *Today* involved hard

news. My job was to administer a questionnaire about the effi-
cacy of *Parade* magazine, a vapid Sunday insert featuring household hints and peppy interviews with noncontroversial celebrities. Beginning with the *A*'s in the white pages, I quizzed locals
willing to give me ten or fifteen minutes, and because so many
women then stayed home with small children, they almost
always picked up, welcoming the break in their routine. "Which
Parade feature do you turn to first?" I asked, as, against a background of shrieking toddlers and barking dogs, the interviewee
ducked gratefully into a bedroom and composed her languid
reply: "Now, let's see. Ah always like when they write about
pies." On I went, politely, asking about cover stories, advice col-
umns, ads. Occasionally I reached a man, who might praise an
item about a scientific breakthrough that had been covered elsewhere three months before, or an article on which kind of lawn-
mower to buy. I found the work pleasant, because people were
so nice, and I had a valid excuse to stay on the phone all day.

The next summer, having noticed my ease with the telephone, Dad recommended me to the ABC ("A Better Choice")
Answering Service, which covered his calls. The company,
owned and run by a single mother out of her second-floor apartment, had about thirty clients, represented in the living room
by a long bank of wall telephones mounted on plywood sheets,
two rows of them, each phone topped by the business name
and a tiny light bulb so one could pick out the active lines by
sight. Working for ABC was as simple as babysitting. All I did
was lounge in a recliner and wait for one of the phones to ring.
I'd answer with the business name and jot a message on a pink
"While You Were Out" slip provided on a long, lunch-count-
er-type desk bolted to the wall beneath the phones. On slow
days, a whole hour might pass in silence, and I could read, unin-
terrupted. Occasionally, though, I had to manage several near-

simultaneous rings, leaping out of the La-Z-Boy and grabbing at receivers from one end of the wall to the other, begging callers to hold on while I disentangled myself from the receiver wires, the stout, curly type with which criminals on TV bound their victims.

I liked my boss, a tall sturdy woman with an intense, professional focus. Dorie was one of the most direct women I'd ever met—nearly mannish by the standards of femininity I was absorbing from *Mademoiselle* and *Glamour*—and since I drank that Kool-Aid with every issue, I thought Dorie's forthright demeanor might be why she was divorced; she hadn't been girlish enough for her husband. I was surprised, then, when a polite, good-looking fellow from Miami started dropping in, and I was called to work not just when Dorie took time with her ten-year-old daughter, but when she went out on a date and the daughter was sent to a friend's house to play. Once, Dorie forgot what time she'd asked me to arrive, and when I pushed open the front door, I heard her cry from the bedroom, "Who's there?" and the sound of bodies rising from a groaning mattress. "Wait, please," she called, and I stood, unmoving, before the thirty wall phones. Even in our thin-walled home, I'd never heard such an indicator from my parents' bedroom. After an interval, Dorie and her boyfriend emerged, dressed, as if nothing had happened, and departed for dinner. Toward the end of my tenure at ABC, I learned, through some overheard snippet of conversation, that Dorie's boyfriend was married and realized that what I thought was an adult courtship was a doomed affair. I concluded that being a take-charge female led to limited relationships with men; that such a woman might have some fun now and then, but would ultimately remain alone. I was slow to admire Dorie's resourcefulness, offering a service from home that connected her to the business world, a bold move for a single mother in the early 1960s. Nor did I immediately pick up on her discretion with regard to her daughter. In a small, gossipy family town, a quiet affair with someone from a city 150 miles away may have been Dorie's best opportunity at private intimacy. She must have trusted my own discretion, or anyway, she should have, because I never mentioned it to anyone, not even my parents.

❲ ❲ ❲

White Acres was a five-minute walk to Draa Field, the community football stadium bracketed on one side by new open-air seating, steel-framed, with bolted wooden seats, and on the other by soaring, covered wooden baseball bleachers that held several hundred fans in raked rows, as within a movie theater. That forest green antique, built when Draa *was* a baseball diamond, backed to the street, so passing it, one had the impression of an enormous hunchback leaning over the games. At night, it frightened me, like dreams of a haunted house.

Titusville had two high schools in the early 1960s: Titusville High, white, and Gibson High, black, and both used Draa Field. Living so close, we heard football crowds roar all weekend, as Gibson's games took place Friday nights, and Titusville High's games Saturdays, with junior high games falling in the afternoons. On Friday evenings, the first year or two, I rode my bicycle to the field, stopping at the chain link behind the west goal posts to watch Gibson's games. Here, there was no gate—the entrance and refreshment bar stood at the east end—and so, no supervision. From this vantage point, I could see into the covered bleachers where the hometown audience sat, watch more dark faces than I'd ever seen gathered, thrill to the constant movement, the buoyant shouts and piercing whistles far more exuberant than a white crowd's. Gibson's cheerleaders,

clad in bright blue and red skirts and letter sweaters, led routines
I committed to memory and, back home, repeated to myself in
wonder: "We's for the red, we's for the blue—Come on, Gibson,
we's for YOU!" My favorite cheer was paired with a shocking
bump and grind: "Up my tail, down my spine—Boogity, boogity, hold that line!" I taught it to my sister, and we tried to imitate the Gibson cheerleaders, half mocking, half envious.

After forty-five years, it's hard to explain a white girl's fas-
cination with black people at the dawn of the civil rights era.
Before we moved to Titusville, I'd met only a few African
Americans: occasional, pleasant employees around the Wash-
ington neighborhood, and two women associated with Mom's
United Fund volunteer work in Fort Lauderdale.

I had watched other black people at gas stations in central
and north Florida, and on vacations to North Carolina, as they
rounded a corner to the Colored Only rest room, drank from
the Colored Only fountain. Perhaps because my parents didn't
make racist remarks or openly address racial issues, I remained
naive, unable to articulate the social divisions I noticed. Black
people were Other, and mostly poorer, it seemed, but were
they so Other they required separate water fountains? What
alien germs could they possibly leave behind? Here in the Deep
South, I sensed complex fears attached to them—their own,
that of whites, and mine, which were mixed with curiosity, the
kind embedded in an inner challenge to break through something, to *understand* it.

During our first spring in town, 1963, the Southern Christian Leadership Conference, Dr. Martin Luther King, and others led the historic nonviolent Birmingham campaign, and in
June, President Kennedy endorsed civil rights in a televised
speech; hours later, NAACP field secretary Medgar Evers was
assassinated in Mississippi. Suddenly, those of us living in small

Southern communities wondered what might erupt across town or down the street. Although newcomers like us weren't aware of it, Titusville, in its Confederate days home to black market action and a wartime salt works, had a history of racial problems, notably the KKK's 1951 Christmas Eve bombing of black activist Harry Tyson Moore's home in Mims, a village north of town where some Space Center employees bought homes. Moore had founded the Brevard County branch of the NAACP in 1934 and spent years working for black voter registration, equal pay for black teachers, better housing and education in Florida. (Not until 2004 did the county create a memorial to Moore on his home site.)

One hundred miles north of Titusville, after Medgar Evers's death, Robert B. Hayling, a Saint Augustine dentist and NAACP advisor, led demonstrations, firing up members of the Florida Klan and other whites, who took to violence. In August 1963, the March on Washington for Jobs and Freedom took place, culminating in Dr. King's "I Have a Dream" speech. Violence in Saint Augustine continued. A grand jury blamed Hayling, among others, and the NAACP asked for Hayling's resignation. In September, four black girls were killed by a bomb in a Birmingham Baptist church. In November, the president was shot.

If the Klan was active in Brevard County, it wasn't mentioned in the *Star-Advocate*. Racial news was still elsewhere, up the coast. Now, Saint Augustine's blacks had turned to the SCLC and Dr. King, who questioned the White House's support of the city's upcoming four-hundredth birthday celebration. Blacks and whites joined in a massive nonviolent movement in the city that went on for months. Of this, I remember June 11, 1964, when Dr. King was arrested for trespassing at a whites-only motel restaurant, and the eighteenth, when blacks and whites staged an integrated swim-in at the same motel, and the manager poured muriatic acid into the pool in an effort to get them out. (The acid, so diluted, was harmless.) Two weeks later, July 2, the Civil Rights Act of 1964 was enacted. Historical records show the Florida KKK stepped up its efforts exactly then.

In Titusville, I discovered early on, there was a clear line—South Street—between the white and black neighborhoods. The presence of a notorious bar, the Orange and Green, fronting the black side, added an element of fright, as if its very existence guaranteed a riot. The summer I learned to drive, 1966, a friend wanting to scare me, asked, "What if you ran out of gas in front of the *Orange and Green*?" Why, I thought, the men loitering out front would descend on me and I'd have to beg a barmaid to help! Yet I have a memory of tottering to a dead stop in front of the *Orange and Green*, and being immediately assisted by a couple of patrons—good angels, after all! Could it have been a fantasy?

Some Titusville citizens generated troubling, and lightly reported, events: a racial disturbance at the Magnolia Theater, and another at Draa Field, reportedly enflamed by adults; there were attacks on the Sand Drift Youth Center for alleged membership discrimination, and plans for an all-white Christian school. After several incidents, Titusville's town fathers formed a "human relations commission," ostensibly to deal with racial problems. But in 1968, a report by the Urban Research Center charged that Titusville and its city leaders were "not in tune" with the times. Yes, there had been an Equal Rights parade—my parents marched in it—but on the whole, Titusville was, like many other Southern towns, unwilling, or at best slow, to change.

《 《 《

In 1966–67, my sophomore year of high school, Titusville
schools were partially integrated, and in my junior year, Titusville and Gibson High combined as one campus, the two lying
literally across the railroad tracks from each other; students
walked back and forth between them, according to class sched-
ules. By then, I was so fixated on my brilliant music career I
only noticed—or only remember—integration's impact within
the band, notably in the marching drum line. With former Gibson students in the rhythm section, the British military cadences
taught by our director, Mr. Courson, a Wagner-loving baritone
horn player, were swept out overnight and there was nothing
he could do about it. All of us, black and white, loved Gibson
High's loosely swung patterns, the rock emphasis on off-beats
that turned knee-jerk Sousa into half-time soul. Soon, instead
of pivoting smartly for a left turn step into tight formation, we
were twirling 180 degrees, one leg cocked, pumping our instru-
ments high in the air like first-place trophies. The crowd at Draa
Field hollered and screamed as if the band, not the team, had
taken the game. Nobody could resist that. Nobody.

I was hardly the only white student freed up by the new
marching style. One boy, a brooding, bespectacled saxophone
player known for his prowess in calculus and chess, surprised
everyone by volunteering to lead a platoon, and within the week
could be heard on the field screaming at his charges to "Step
high, play loud, rock out!" If the results failed to satisfy, his volume intensified: "Did you HEAR me, people? ROCK OUT!
ROCK OUT! ROCK OUT!" Even the collective pulse of my
own platoon, one down from his, quickened at the sound of
his voice and the shock of Michael's incredible transformation
from nervous scholar to fiery exhorter. "All right, listen up," I'd
shout to my line of seven, all girls, all clarinet players, whose

thin, wheezy tones would be obliterated by Michael's belting saxes, "Do it like you mean it—rock out!" And together, we'd jut the right knee straight into the sun, plant that foot flat into the sand, and let our hips go soft in come-hither rolls as we proceeded ahead: left, BOOM, right, BOOM, left—resembling, for the first time on the field, the women we were becoming.

But in the rehearsal room, black and white relations weren't always smooth. My own crisis took place one autumn, when band members were peddling bars of World's Finest Chocolate to earn money for a spring trip. Mr. Courson posted our individual profits weekly, encouraging a contest, and I was top seller that year, having developed a strategy aimed at hungry classmates. Although most of my peers wouldn't drop fifty cents for chocolate, many could spare a dime or quarter, so during classes like Geometry or World History, I, seated toward the back, chopped World's Finest's foil-wrapped ingots with a nail file into bargain segments and passed them along underhand, my ears alert to the soft clink of loose change some seats away, my fingers hanging in the air to receive payment. I was the queen of band candy marketing.

In the midst of the candy drive, Mom took me shopping in Orlando, and in the Colonial Shopping Center I fell upon an excellent navy blue vinyl knockoff of an expensive leather and tweed handbag like the moneyed girls carried. About twelve inches square, and large enough to hold a billfold, compact, hairbrush, and a spare Kotex, its "leather" straps were affixed to the nubby fabric face with gold-tone grommets, a touch repeated at the four corners of the bag's bottom. The authentic purses, more often rendered with oxblood leather trim (but available in blue, I knew) bore horseshoe closures, referencing the style's equestrian attitude, an indication of social class. The imitation I gazed upon, which had a simple twist latch, not a horseshoe, was the closest I would get to owning a fashionable bag, and from a distance, you couldn't tell the difference. I spent everything I had on it—five dollars—elated at my great fortune, congratulating myself on my discriminating eye. When we got home, I immediately poured everything from my old purse into the new one, including a fat envelope containing $75 in band candy profits, due at school after the weekend. On Monday, sometime between the moment I stepped into the band hall and the end of rehearsal, when we were to deliver our candy proceeds to Mr. Courson, someone swiped my faux-equestrian bag.

How could it have vanished? There had to be a mistake. The purse must be in the room. Shrugging the fresh sweat nicking down my back, I cast back to the start of the period, watched myself stride purposefully to the instrument shelf, clutching the prized handbag with the right hand, setting it down, drawing my clarinet case from its slot in the lineup, and—what? The picture muddied. Naturally, I had slung the purse up my right arm and held the instrument handle with the left hand. Yes. And I had brought everything to my seat, stowed my purse beneath it, opened my case, and assembled my instrument.

Maybe someone had kicked the pocketbook under an adjacent chair. I checked, and found nothing. Or I'd forgotten it, and left it on the instrument shelf. No. What about that table next to the conductor's podium that served as a lost and found? Nothing there. Finally, I approached Mr. Courson: had he seen a purse that looked like . . . ? No. And because Mr. Courson had already retreated into his trademark silence, his visage a marble bust of Wagner, I said nothing and stumbled out, dizzy with shock.

In tears, I told my parents, who buoyed me with anger at the unknown thief—a relief, because I'd expected a warning about carelessness. The next day we all conferred with Mr. Courson. How should the lost candy money, not a small sum then, be replaced? I wasn't good for it—my entire personal savings of $5 had gone for the purse. I don't recall how it was settled, but someone or something bailed me out, and I was allowed to retain my sales lead, continuing to clean up on partial chocolate bars when my teachers weren't looking, building my account, yet at the same time writhing over the loss of that pocketbook. For it was not just the purse I'd lost, but the satisfaction of having discovered it and passed it off as the real thing—a minor blessing. How quickly a tidbit of perceived magic could disappear, as if it had never occurred.

About a week after the incident, in rehearsal, I was blaring away with everyone else on a memorized showstopper, probably "Hello, Dolly"—every marching band in the state of Florida was mad with it—when my eyes fell on a purse—my purse—at the feet of a tall black girl in the bass clarinet section. The girl felt my eyes, and without so much as a turn aside from her mouthpiece, stared back in a sure challenge. My stomach pitched, and I looked away. No one wanted any trouble, especially the white majority school administration, and we both knew it. "Incidents," though not always reported widely, were common. And now that the purse snatcher's identity had been confirmed, albeit privately, a great wave of suppressed anguish rose up in me, not simply over the loss of the prized purse, but the unjust debt incurred by those who'd bailed me out, my guilt over it, the silent undercutting of my sales lead, and the sense I was unlikely to get any justice in the matter. As well, I imagined the girl might have really needed the money, and wouldn't it have been tempting to take the extra cash that self-important blond clarinet player was carrying around? Now I felt uneasy about my advantage—my privilege as a white person.

Still, after the brassy, triumphant finish of "Hello, Dolly"

("Dolly will never go away again!"), I reported to Mr. Courson, who asked if I was sure the purse was mine. "Yes," I said. "No one else has one like it." And I explained how friends—friends understandably reticent to back me up—admired the blue "leather" as opposed to the more common saddle brown: a weak argument, I knew, from a shallow point of view. A school administrator, white, was called to the conversation. "Did your purse have any identifying marks?" he asked. "A particular scratch or other sign of wear?" "No—it was brand new," I said. "Well then," he said. "It *could* be hers. Best not to say anything." And no one did. For the rest of the school year, from the toe-tapping Hello Dolly halftime show to the concerted siege of Wagner's "Invocation of Alberich"—in which we sunburned kids, ignorant of mythology, attempted to dramatize the dwarf king's forging of a cursed ring—the tall girl openly carried the purse, and between us, we carried the secret knowledge of her triumph.

《 《 《

If I was blind to the subtle movements of racial power then, I was also blind to skin color, in a particular instance. Sometime after the purse incident, a trumpet player told me his friend Gene, a saxophone player, wanted to take me out on a date. I was floored. I did not date, had repressed most interest since my first and last junior high dance, for which Mom had commissioned a local seamstress to sew me a bright yellow dress and matching jacket—an embarrassment, when I got to the dance and saw everyone in their school clothes. I supposed she was thinking of 1930s Bangor. The few boys who had asked me out were several years older than I, and my mother refused to let me go with all but one, a bashful friend of the family who, when he delivered me home after the basketball game, hugged me and patted me on the back, as if comforting a weeping child. The only other markers of a love life were a necking session in the Magnolia Theater's back row with a tuba player who made out with everybody, and a kiss in the bushes at a pool party, interrupted by a mosquito truck spraying DDT fog into the hedge, after which the boy decided it would be more fun to pull up a street sign and throw it into the pool. I bore a long succession of one-sided crushes, marked by exclamation points in my diaries like spikes in barometric pressure, and had grown used to, and grateful for, the band's camaraderie, which fed me socially, postponing or flattening the desire for a special Other. Now, someone my age wanted to pick me up in his car and treat me to what—a school dance? A movie? I was excited, but unprepared. I wouldn't know what to do if what—he held my hand? Tried to kiss me? Who was Gene, anyway? I thought I knew everyone in the band.

"Look at the sax section in rehearsal tomorrow," David said. "You'll see him."

And I did look, studying the familiar faces, one by one: Michael, Sandy, Greg . . . passing over new black countenances like empty spaces on a library bookshelf.

"Did you see him?" David asked afterward, eager to make the match.

"No," I said. "I don't know who you're talking about."

"Try again," David said, and I did, but the results were the same.

On the third day, after rehearsal, a handsome black fellow appeared at my elbow. "Ann?" he said. "I'm Gene."

He might as well have leaped naked from behind a shower curtain. I was still reeling from the purse incident, fighting to overcome the feeling that all the black kids might really have it in for the whites. That, and the fact that a black beau had never occurred to me. But I understood Gene was warm and friendly, and, aware that my reaction might be taken as revulsion (base fear was bad enough), I stepped forward. Gene offered his hand, and I shook it.

"It's nice to meet you," I said, and meant it, and went home to spend a tortured evening ruminating over the situation.

I liked Gene and was flattered by his interest, even though I had heard a white girl in gym class say black boys only wanted us as trophies. I didn't believe it. But going out with Gene would be more than going out with Gene—it would be the first interracial date I was aware of, sure to incite discussion at school, in the community. I doubted my parents would approve. My father, despite years away from his country upbringing (I'd heard his least-traveled, least-educated brother use the "n" word), and because he knew how provincial towns worked, would have said no, for it might have put our family in danger. My mother, open-minded but protective and good at deploying practical reasoning for agreeable ends, would have suggested I might not want the social burden this one date would bestow. Huddled alone in my bed, channeling the couple sleeping soundly on the other side of the wall, I decided they were right, even though I hadn't said a word to them.

The next morning between classes, I ran into David.

"So—would you go out with Gene?" he asked.

"No, no," I said. He's a great guy, but—no, I can't."

"It's OK," David said, kindly. "He understands."

I nodded with relief, suddenly caught Gene's eyes across the hall, and saw he'd watched the exchange. He nodded back at me. At that moment, I wished I'd been courageous enough to say "yes" to him. I was ashamed of and confused by my complicated response, and for some time regretted it, as Gene seemed to navigate the halls with ease, grew popular with both blacks and whites, and was elected senior class secretary. He was far more socially adept than I, the canny candy sales queen, lurking behind books and music with her nail file and chocolates. He had begun to cross the divide, whereas I had not.

Yet in the same year, other white students and I were cajoled, and occasionally shoved forward by Robert Manning, a young, black Sociology teacher who practiced sensitivity training. Early on, he strode in with a tall stack of *Ebony* magazines and passed them out to our all-white class, so each student had one. "Just take a look," he said. "Enjoy the pictures, read an article or two." There were photographs of black couples in evening gowns and tuxes, attending a banquet! Cigarette advertisements featuring glamorous, dark-skinned models! Special products for thick, curly hair! In a flash, one magazine revealed an entire world I wasn't privy to or had the curiosity to imagine—it seemed another civilization, another planet, and at the same time, it was "just like us." I drifted out of class that day, stunned by the light Mr. Manning had thrown on the people who occupied the homes, churches, and businesses behind the Orange and Green. The light thrown on me. Later on, in PE, I stared at all the black and white skin in the dressing room, decentralizing my vision, trying for blurred caramel, everyone the same. It was too much for my eyes. Yet Mr. Manning's radical opinion, that the only solution to racial strife was complete, planetary amalgamation, could be correct.

III

In 1962, a young woman at the University of Connecticut wrote NASA about becoming an astronaut. The director of public information, O. B. Lloyd, replied, in part: "Your offer to go on a space mission is commendable, and we are very grateful. This is to advise that we have no existing program concerning women nor do we contemplate any such plan." The Russians beat the Americans on that score by twenty years, sending Valentina Tereshkova into the ether in 1963.

In 1964, on my thirteenth birthday, the *Star-Advocate* published the following letter, part of a syndicated advice column:

> Titusville Star-Advocate, July 27, 1964
> Dear Ann Landers:
>
> I'm a 20-year-old blonde who is all mixed up. My dad is a golf pro. I've been playing golf since I was six. I shoot a pretty spectacular game, which is part of my problem. I can cream all the fellows in our crowd—including my steady guy.
>
> Howie hates it when I beat him but I can't do less than my best when I get on the course. I beat Howie at tennis, too, which is rather embarrassing as he considers himself an expert and has taken lessons for years.
>
> I'd like to marry Howie but he becomes so sullen and uncommunicative when he loses to me I wonder if we could have a good life together.
>
> The guy has a dozen marvelous qualities and I'd hate to break up with him because of this one fault. What do you say?
>
> Three Under Par
> Dear Three:
>
> Play doubles with Howie as your partner and make him look good instead of beating his brains out. No more head-on competition. When you win, you lose.

This column encapsulated my own struggle with the boy-girl question. Our family had just traveled to the New York World's

Fair and attended a new Broadway musical recommended by
friends. *Funny Girl* starred an unknown singer named Barbra
Streisand, who, we agreed, was bound for stardom, and I, ever
envisioning a musical career, took "Don't Rain on My Parade"
for my anthem. But four years later, I intentionally screwed up a
statewide audition so my first-ever boyfriend, a clarinet player in
another town, would place higher, even though I'd easily passed
him the previous year, before we'd met. When the auditions
were complete and our positions announced (mine two seats
down from the boy's), a judge who had taught us both at Florida
State's summer music camp drew me aside and asked, "What
were you *doing* in there?"

What *was* I doing? I'd long recovered from the Beethoven
fiasco and at the music camp had begun to discipline my technique. My band uniform was encrusted with competition med-
als; when I walked around in it, I sounded like quarters clank-
ing in a jelly jar. Mom had found a new teacher in town: a
musician who had inexplicably retired to Titusville, a gaunt,
wiry woman (never married, I noted), who had played trombone in an all-women dance band during World War II—the
golden era of those bands, when so many men were off to war.
In Miss T's living room, where she taught, I gawked at framed
black-and-white photographs of this flinty woman in her heyday, decked out in frilly gowns, the trombone at her shoulder
and lips, its slide in her right hand, thrusting high, nigh unto
heaven. She was a humorless taskmaster, Miss T, focused on the
only thing she, a brass player, could confidently require of a clarinetist: arduous scale study, which did help. Up and down the
note ladders I chugged, eyeing the china dogs and cats on her
mantelpiece, the kind with those puzzled, pursed-lip expressions
some people think cute.

After working with Miss T, I received a scholarship to the

Brevard Music Center in North Carolina and studied with Florida State's clarinet professor, Harry Schmidt, a graduate of the New England Conservatory who had established a platform for himself in the South. Harry was enamored of the French school of clarinet playing, which stressed, among other things, lightning facility over depth of tone. Even in the low register, he sounded reedy and desperate, as if itching, always, to move off the mark. But his fingers sure did fly. "Rhythm in the fingers!" he'd cry, as I whipped through etude after etude on a stream of wheezy sound. To relieve stress on a player's right hand, which bore most of the instrument's weight, Mr. Schmidt invented a contraption marketed as the Schmidt Positioner. It consisted of a rod connecting the center joint of the clarinet to a metal plate on the player's chest, and a neck strap that hooked into the chest plate, the object being to free the right hand and transfer stress to the neck. Everyone who studied with Harry had to use it, even if it undermined one's embouchure—the arrangement of lips and teeth on the mouthpiece—a locus of pitch and tone refinement. I felt idiotic wearing it, like a perfectly good dancer saddled with a needless, ugly brace, and it drew the eye to my breasts. At the end of the five-week camp, an acquaintance let it slip that Harry called me, in the presence of male students, Big Peaches.

Where, then, in the 1960s, could a girl of reasonable musical talent find a comfortable niche in what was still a man's world? For me, it appeared in a world of boys that desperately needed a clarinet player. My chance came at Florida State's camp, when a man whose daughter played oboe in my group heard me in a little solo, appeared backstage, and offered me my first paying gig, with a big band of teenage musicians drawn from across Brevard County.

"I'd like you to join us on clarinet. Like Benny Goodman. Do you know boogie-woogie?"

No, I did not know boogie-woogie, but I nodded, and the deal was closed.

The man's son, a high school trumpeter, had started the band, but died soon afterward in a car accident. As a memorial, Mr. Miner led the Silvertones forward, organizing Sunday afternoon rehearsals in his Indialantic Beach living room and booking the group Friday and Saturday nights. The band specialized in hits of the 1930s, '40s, and early '50s; its clients were Space Center aircraft companies like McDonnell Douglas, Boeing, and Bendix, and military venues like the Patrick Air Force Base Officer's Club. Each member of the Silvertones received $20 for a four-hour gig, or $5 an hour—lower than union rate, I learned later, but minimum wage then was $1.25; $5 was gold. After joining the band, I heard whispered references to the local chapter of the American Federation of Musicians. Apparently, the AF of M didn't appreciate the Silvertones, though no one could argue with Mr. Miner's mission.

Two weeks later, Mom drove me the forty-five miles to my first rehearsal because I only had a learner's license. The Miners' home exterior was that of any other midcentury Florida house; through the wide picture window, one would have expected to see rattan furniture and ashtrays. But as we approached the front door, we noticed the furniture had been pushed against the walls or moved out to make space for a dozen big band stands modeled on those seen on the Lawrence Welk show. The Silvertones' were of plywood, painted black, with *S* and *T* in silver. Behind each stand sat a teenaged boy noodling full blast on a saxophone, trumpet, or trombone. Back of the winds, a drummer riffed and intermittently smashed a cymbal; a string bassist thumped bottom. In the far corner, Gayle, Mr. Miner's daughter and the only other girl, struck and rolled chords on an upright piano.

John Miner introduced us to his wife, Ruth, and Mom joined her at the kitchen table, off to the side, to listen. The second tenor sax player, near the left wall, pointed to an empty chair beside him. I scootched and stumbled over instrument cases and several pairs of boys' feet to claim it, and, sweaty palmed, assembled my clarinet. The din died down. Mr. Miner announced I'd joined the band. The boys looked around at me, nodded, gave a little cheer, and a-one-and-a-two, the Silvertones plunged into "Take the A Train," my first big band chart. I faltered and flailed, but caught on fairly quickly. I knew this music from Mom's old records.

The band was tight, the players excellent, stars at various high schools or nearby colleges. I was lucky to come in on clarinet, to be featured on a scant handful of numbers. Most of the time, I doubled the second tenor sax part, hovering beneath the notes of a more experienced player, from whom I learned big band styles and voicings. Weekly rehearsals and gigs with sixteen confident fellows who considered me a colleague, equal, or even a pal, was the best alternative to the misery of not dating. Over the next four years I would crush on every single one of the boys, but never let on; it would have spoiled the magic.

Now, at fifteen, I was a real musician, showing up to weekend jobs in short lace and sequin dresses I designed and sewed on Mom's aging Singer, accessorizing with fishnet stockings, black patent leather high heels, and costume jewelry from Titusville's ho-hum Belk's, a southern dry goods store a few doors down from the bowling alley. After the first year, Gayle and I bought matching outfits, the most notorious our black, floor-length sheaths with sheer capes floating from the shoulders and poppy-sized rhinestone brooches smack at center chest. We ordered them from the Sears catalog. When I turned sixteen, I was allowed to drive myself to rehearsals and gigs all

over the county. Attired in cocktail getups years before I was allowed to drink, I swanked into the employee entrances of an Elk's Club, an Officer's Club, or a city convention center, swinging my instrument case like a lunch pail. At the end of the evening, midnight or 1:00 a.m., Mr. Miner handed each of us a twenty-dollar bill. My first pay I squandered on shampoo and Summer Blonde hair lightener. Later, I opened a savings account at the bank and immediately swung around to the drive-in teller, like a grown-up, I thought, and withdrew five dollars.

After a few weeks doubling the second tenor sax and soloing on transcribed Benny Goodman hits (I never learned to improvise), Mr. Miner took me aside. One of the alto sax players was leaving for college out of state. "You need to get an alto," he said. "We'll put you on second when you're not in a clarinet feature."

I'd never even held a saxophone, but tried a friend's and found it easy to play. Dad took me by Titusville's music store to see what a decent alto would cost me, for as a professional, we agreed, I would purchase it myself. The owner offered a new Vito, a good student instrument, for $150, which I could pay for on time: three installments of $50 each. I could earn that much in eight gigs, the rest of the summer's work.

"I'll draw up the contract," said the man. "But since you're under eighteen, a parent will have to co-sign."

When I looked to my father, his principles popped up, like the metal numbers on an antique cash register. He refused to sign. It was my contract, not his, he said.

"Why does she need my signature, when she's the one buying the saxophone?" he asked the owner. "It doesn't make any sense."

"But sir, Florida law says if an under-age . . ."

"I don't care what the law says," Dad interrupted. "It's her contract, so all you should need is her word. If she defaults, I'm not going to pick up the payment."

"I understand your point of view, sir, but . . ."

"No buts about it," Dad said. "I'm not signing a thing."

We left the store, Dad stern and steaming, I mortified and angry. He didn't *want* me to have the saxophone. He was out to ruin my life.

"Don't you see I can't earn anything without it?" I cried. "The Silvertones want me to play the saxophone."

"I thought they wanted you for clarinet."

"That was to start. But now . . ."

"I understand. But I'm not going to sign. It's your loan." And then he added what I knew was coming: "It's the principle of the thing."

He could be so wrongheaded for his perfectly good reasons.

Mom, so skillful at reasoning with her husband and interpreting him to their daughters, stepped in, and one of them, probably her, cosigned the loan. Off I went to a summer of gigs. I covered the first two payments with ease, proudly delivering cash to the music store, but when two August jobs were canceled, I saw I wouldn't make the final payment. I confided this to Mom. It was July, and my birthday was coming up. Her present to me was the exact amount I owed, and I would bet good money Dad didn't realize it. Later, I wondered if his stubbornness in the situation reflected his age, as well as his principles. It was the first time I noticed he was a generation older than my friends' fathers. Recently, an old neighbor said he'd talked about sending me to a home for wayward girls, and when I laughed, she insisted he hadn't been joking. Now I see how fast the times, and his daughter, were slipping away from him.

《 《 《

The saxophone episode occurred the summer of 1966, a few months after the postwar economy stumbled. The gig cancellations were probably related, and this is when Dad's optimism about the future seemed to slip; perhaps it extended to concern about my loan, for in the past, he hadn't hesitated to cover my music expenses—it was he who had given me my first professional model clarinet, writing on the Christmas tag, "Don't let anyone with a cheap clarinet beat you out." By now, though, he might have realized two reasons why Titusville had not been a wise choice for a new business, even though it was closest to the Space Center's northern entrance and the launchpads. Of the Space towns, it was, culturally, the most resistant to change— which he might not have known, and the only one without an accessible public beach—which he might not have taken fully into account, not being a swimmer or sun worshipper. He may

have been thinking, instead, of optimal commuting time. As
it turned out, more incoming families wanted proximity to the
ocean, where fun in the sun was a short walk away, and property
values were soaring. Many of the professional class, such as doctors and lawyers, settled in Cocoa or Melbourne and commuted
to satellite offices in Titusville. Now I sensed an undercurrent of
anxiety, a nameless tension. My father's resting expression, usually pleasant, had begun to droop.

My sister and I both noticed it. Every so often, Dad unexpectedly flew off the handle about something—had an overre-
action, we'd say today, akin to his earlier response to my overdue book. There were a few physical outbursts: a slap of his belt
for talking back, and once the beating of our dog, Jonas, who
on a clear summer night would not stop barking at the moon.
This incident, the mistreatment of an innocent animal, struck
me hardest. Although Dad never hit Jonas again, he'd turned
an innocent animal into one that bit. Soon afterward, a friend
invited me on a church bus excursion to Daytona Beach, where
we were shown a movie in which a teenager in dire straits turns
his life over to Christ. Annoyed by the propaganda, I remained
cool and detached, until the end, when the hero broke down in
tears. Something loosened in me, and with the inevitable altar
call, I rose and accepted the hand of a smiling guide, who led
me to a corner backstage. "Will you pray to accept Jesus Christ
as your savior?" the woman asked. "No," I said. "I want to pray
for my father."

《 《 《

It seemed everything had to be spotlessly clean, a blank canvas on which to project something new, new, NEW, and this
extended to a girl's complexion. But if I thought I was the only

girl picking pimples, the deep bank of Clearasil products down
at the Rexall set me straight. Titusville's burgeoning family population included hundreds of teens—my high school class numbered over 650—and a lot of us relied on the flesh-hued com-
pound that sat up on a pimple, a pert dab of spackle announcing
to the world that one layer down, Vesuvius was about to erupt.
A year or two after we moved to Titusville, someone opened a
Merle Norman cosmetic studio and every girl over twelve and
her mother signed up for the free facial and makeup lesson, followed by a sales pitch and the unmistakable obligation to buy
something. I acquired a tub or two of the putty-like foundation,
but recall most vividly a pore-tightening mask named Miracol,
a pink-orange solution applied with a brush. As Miracol dried,
it grew shiny and pulled the skin this way and that, according
to the vagaries of brushwork, so that one resembled a burn victim. If you happened to laugh while so anointed, a crazed effect
broke out around the nose, mouth, and cheeks, as in a ceramic
project gone wrong. The stuff did burn, bringing one to tears
and satisfying those who believed pain indicated improvement;
one laugh-shattering rendered a girl so grotesque that once the
mask was scrubbed away, her own, unchanged face appeared
beautiful, transformed.

If Miracol failed to rid a Titusville girl of pimples, her
mother might trot her down to a dermatologist in Cocoa, as
mine did. Every few weeks, for months, I donned protective
goggles and submitted myself to an ultraviolet lamp, each session leaving me looking as if I'd lain beneath a Saturn V during
takeoff. With more frequent trips to the beach, I could have
accomplished the same ravaged peeling and called it cool. But
if my face was my obsession, my hair was my cross to bear. The
modest locks, thin and baby fine like my father's, failed every

morning to "behave," as ads used to speak of it, and I fell, with
descending hopes, for all the products: Aqua Net hair spray
smelling of bug repellant, green Dippity-Do styling gel that
slimed your temples, and dyes that promised "full body" and
"uplift," as if a head of hair was a sad, deflated old thing requiring daily resuscitation or life support. A peroxide lightener
singed my hair to straw; the henna-based dyes slid out, fickle as
soap, taking me from Deep Chestnut back to mousy in weeks.
And still, I coveted that stiff space helmet 'do every girl had to
have, turning myself over to Bill at Bill's House of Beauty, who
cut every head in town exactly the same way before the single mirror in his Baldwin Shopping Plaza salon. It's not difficult
to return to that chair, stare at my anxious face amid the plastic roses encircling the mirror, and watch Bill, a fortyish pixie
flitting about with comb and scissors, chattering as quickly as
a sandpiper skitters, his sour old mother watching silently from
the faux French provincial desk, waiting to ring up the charges.

The House of Beauty repeatedly failed me, so when Wigs
'n' Things over by Searstown Mall fell victim to a conflagra-
tion and held a fire sale, I was first in line with my Silvertones
pay. Into that charred vault I crept, scanning wigs for something
that could look like mine, if I had thick hair, but it was useless, for even a smoked Lady Godiva was out of my price range.
As if cued, the owner behind the cash register hollered, "How
'bout a wiglet?" and I followed her sausage arm as she gestured
toward a wall of splayed hair hanks, pinned down like varmints
that might escape and bite. In the dim light, I selected one to
match my poor tresses, and handed the proprietor twenty dollars. At home, I discovered what a bad match I'd made, and
that the wiglet stank of ashes. I shampooed the thing, leaving
it on a Styrofoam brainpan to dry, and pinned it into my Aqua
Net helmet for a gig that evening. It looked pretty good. But as

I crossed the Melbourne Convention Center stage beneath an active air vent, I smelled charcoal, and it was me.

And the diets. First, starvation, then grapefruit, nearly as cheap as starvation, because there was a grove just outside town where you could pick up a sack for pennies. Other diets followed, published in the newspaper or passed from friend to friend on faded mimeographs. All we had to do was drink a little of this, eat a little of that, and our fat would evaporate as we slept. The biggest gyp was the vibrating belt machine, a contraption promising to shake away pounds of butt, as the hopeful user stood passively on a little platform, encircled at the hips by a motorized strap. The local rent-all touted these, and once, I purchased a two-day contract, lugging the thing home in the Falcon's trunk. I spent most of a weekend agitating my backside, measuring my hips at intervals. Nothing changed except my kidneys, which lurched into overdrive.

Ear piercing, however, was the most radical beauty move. My parents said only sleazy girls did it, and I'd better not. But at my sixteenth birthday slumber party, a girl named Claudia did the honors for several of us, using one of Mom's sewing machine needles and an ice cube. Eager to transgress again, we searched the cupboards for my parents' single liquor bottle: a dusty gift carafe of crème de menthe they'd never opened. "How do you make a cocktail?" someone asked. "You mix that with fruit juice," came an answer. Grapefruit juice was all we had. We stirred the concoction, took a sip, squealed "Ewww!" and poured it down the sink.

❨ ❨ ❨

Some of these details are jotted, or at least evoked, in the diaries I continued to accumulate. From town to town, from chapter to chapter, the turtle carries her house of words. But once written, the turtle rarely returns to them; much of the writing was for its own sake, or immediate use, not a record, and a lot never made it into the journals, the letters to Lydia, for example.

I named Lydia after the mysterious heroine of Kenneth Roberts's *Lydia Bailey*, the novel I was reading when the need for her arose. When I had a problem, I wrote a letter to Lydia, and then, as Lydia, I replied to myself with an older mentor's advice. How fortunate I was that Lydia was always at hand, ready to dispense sensible, encouraging counsel, to cheer me on. Although her first responses were a bit chirpy, reminiscent of *American Girl* copy, she knew, before I did, that any wisdom one might possess was only as good as the distance she could put between herself and a situation.

That I had devised a way to ground myself, to access part of me that already existed, never occurred to me, and Lydia wasn't me, to me, yet. She was Lydia. No doubt her formal forebears were Ann Landers and Dear Abby, her earliest point of view, my mother's. But she was my ally, and mine alone: I could confess to her thoughts I wouldn't reveal to anyone else. "The stability of the interior environment is the condition for the free and independent life," wrote French physiologist Claude Bernard. Through words and music, it seems I was negotiating two new worlds—a Southern town, and my adolescence—and trying to create an environment, an inner landscape in which I could stand firmly and wander freely with a steady gait.

IV

On the morning of Thursday, January 26, 1967, Titusville woke to news as devastating, locally, as that of President Kennedy's death: the three astronauts tapped for the AS-204 mission, Apollo's first piloted flight, had perished in a flash fire in the Apollo/Saturn command module during a training exercise. They were Roger Chaffee, who had looked forward to his first space flight; Lieutenant Colonel Edward H. White, pilot of *Gemini 4* and the first American to walk in space; and Virgil "Gus" Grissom, veteran of both the Mercury-Redstone and Gemini programs, and a member of the Original Seven astronauts selected in 1959. Grissom would have commanded the first Apollo flight.

Many residents had known the astronauts personally or worked in close proximity to them out at the cape. All of us, young and old, knew their faces well; Grissom was especially familiar, having appeared in *Life* magazine early on, and though he lacked John Glenn's classic good looks, he struck one as the most boyish, ebullient of the group—the one who smiled with his eyes.

The official investigation reported that conditions during the test were "extremely hazardous" but had not been recognized as such, and so, proper safety precautions had not been made.

"There appears to be no adequate explanation for the failure to recognize the test being conducted at the time of the accident as hazardous," the report said. "the only explanation offered the committee is that NASA officials believe they had eliminated all sources of ignition and since to have a fire requires an ignition source, combustible materials, and oxygen, NASA believes that necessary and sufficient action had been taken to prevent a fire.

"Of course, all ignition sources had not been eliminated."

The report concluded the tragedy would set the Apollo program back, perhaps preventing an American moon landing by the magic year everyone was fixed upon: 1969. But, "The target date was and still is essential to efficient management of the program . . . any program and particularly the largest and most comprehensive research and development program ever undertaken by man—the Apollo program—must have scheduled goals."

NASA renamed AS-204 Apollo 1, in honor of Grissom, White, and Chaffee. In 1968, a concerted run-up to Apollo 11 began, with Apollo 7 (October 11), then 8 (December 21, 1968), 9, (March 3, 1969), and 10 (May 18, 1969). Tension and excitement were palpable all over town. At Titusville High, fire drills were often timed to coincide with daytime launches. Students filed out of the 1927 Spanish-style school or from the many portable buildings brought in to accommodate us, stood outdoors and watched the rockets go, right across the river. At First Methodist, and presumably every other church in Titusville, prayers for the astronauts and all space program workers intensified. Out at the cape, NASA chaplain John Stout, a personal friend of Edward White, founded the Apollo Prayer League, a global organization that prayed for the astronauts and worked toward its own lunar goal: to land microfilmed Bibles on the Moon.

☾ ☾ ☾

"Fly Me to the Moon," "Moon River," "Blue Moon," "It's Only a Paper Moon," "Moonlight Serenade," "How High the Moon"—all were increasingly requested at parties and banquets for NASA contractors and military personnel. Now that I was a seasoned member of the Silvertones, I watched with amusement from behind the curved neck of my saxophone the choreography of nodding, turning heads at a table for eight, the way crowd volume directly corresponded with the amount of alcohol consumed. Always, someone wobbled on stage for a speech celebrating a company accomplishment, to great belly roars, whoops, and applause. As the noise crescendoed, the band, signaled by the MC, plunged into a frenzied "One O'Clock Jump," "Stompin' at the Savoy," or "Woodchopper's Ball," propelling everybody to the dance floor. Ties shook, skirts whirled, shoes whizzed straight from feet to baseboards. Once, a man escorting a woman in a wheelchair managed a nail-biting jitterbug, he twirling her about by her left arm as she wheelied expertly with her right. And there was the man who dipped his wife so far back her wig, a streaked Dynel number, vaguely familiar, dropped off, leaving her skin-headed and screaming with laughter.

And in Titusville: Moonlight Drive-In, Moon Islander restaurant, Moon Drive-In Theater. The first, a fifties-style drive-up milkshake and flame-broiled burger joint, opened in 1964. Like Apollo Insurance and Mortgage, it was a family dream calculated to succeed in the boomtown. (It is still in business.) The Moon Islander restaurant, decorated in Florida's ubiquitous Tiki Modern, was a favorite prom destination. One Moon Islander waitress was known to serve frozen daiquiris to teens as "a special dessert." The Moon Drive-In, Titusville's X-rated theater, was notable for its owner: a popular classmate's father. The night I sneaked into the Moon, flattened against the backseat floorboards of an older friend's car, I was shocked to see that classmate working the ticket booth in a crisp shirtwaist. I never sneaked again; besides, one could view the screen for free from a vacant lot in the adjacent housing development.

At the start of my high school years, I struck up with Leslie, a friend who was neither musically trained nor literary, but bright and funny and willing to slack off with me, driving around town munching animal crackers and sucking Slurpees from the 7-Eleven, singing along with the radio. It appeared we had little else in common. She found school a challenge, while I increasingly blew it off. She joined the Girl Scouts, while I stood by and smirked. She was devoted to an old-school Texas grandmother in thrall to the red letter Bible; my Maine grandmother, now officially diabetic, sneaked chocolates and trounced her grandchildren at cribbage with no apologies. Leslie was the perfect friend for a transitory time, good-natured and accommodating. That her father had worked with Wernher von Braun in Huntsville, had managed Chrysler's work on the Saturn 1B, including electrical wiring for the first stage of all Saturn missiles, those that put Neil Armstrong on the moon, escaped me. The walls of their family den were filled with framed citations, mission patches, and signed photographs of astronauts, and I took them for granted, having seen such displays in other

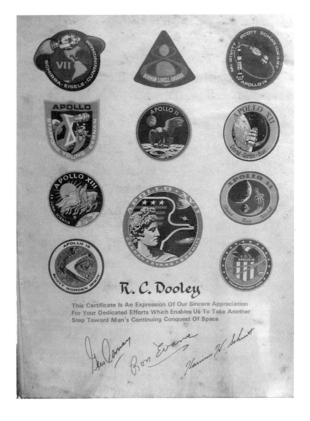

homes. Leslie and I never spoke of her father's work, nor of the space program. We simply shared the need for a good-hearted pal, equally ignorant of our peers' social lives. We'd never been to something called Teen Town, where our classmates danced on weekends. We hadn't been tapped for school clubs or sororities. We didn't know any local bands, not even the Allman Joys in Daytona Beach, who morphed into the Allman Brothers our senior year. We were totally clueless.

In 1967, Titusville celebrated its centennial, the one hundredth anniversary, approximately, of the day Colonel Henry Titus either (a) sailed into an Indian River hamlet called Sand Point and determined to build a town there, (b) was shipwrecked nearby and forced to land, or (c) other. The town held a spring parade; Leslie marched with the Girl Scouts in official dress, carrying a flag; I tramped with the band in my 100 percent wool uniform with the stiff, heavy epaulets, yards of gold braid, and a blue and white hat the size of an ice bucket topped with a gold plume. Band members had complained about these uniforms for years. Even if you wore nothing beneath them but a bikini, you risked heatstroke. The argument for them seemed to be durability and thrift; properly cleaned and stored in airtight plastic during summer, they'd last for decades, safe from Florida's mildew and vermin.

Although Leslie, my sister, and our friends now referred to our town familiarly as Tidyville, Tittyville or Tightassville, as if we owned its story, we had no knowledge of its history until the town's centennial, when the *Star-Advocate* and various event programs proudly revealed Colonel Titus's biography. The town founder was a New Jersey native, born in 1815, 1822, or 1823. He attended West Point, but failed to graduate. Before he arrived in Florida, he had been a postal inspector in Philadelphia, a leader in Narciso López's charge to liberate Cuba from

Spain, a grocery and sawmill operator, an agent of pro-slavery forces in Kansas, a member of William Walker's military expeditions into Latin America, a mine operator in Arizona, a member of the Florida militia during the Civil War, and a supplier to the Confederate Army. After he sailed or washed up at Sand Point, he laid out a town on land his wife owned, erected some buildings, and in 1873, in a game of dominoes, won the right to name the place after himself. He was the quintessential Florida opportunist, operating a hotel in two wings of his house.

In 1885, a new spur off the railroad line from Jacksonville to Tampa ran to Titusville, straight to the Indian River, where steamships still plied the waters. This pleased Titus and other coastal settlers who hoped to cash in on the state's new resort trade. But Titusville missed out on all the hoopla for two reasons. First, a landowner refused railroad magnate Henry Flagler's offer for sixty-seven acres, which Flagler intended to develop as a major resort. The landowner, hoping to strike it rich, set an excessive price, and Flagler, who had other choices, simply went down to Palm Beach.

The other reason Titusville missed out was its great quantity of mosquitoes.

Even so, nineteenth-century wayfarer C. Vickerstaff Rine wrote of the town, "And a fresh little metropolis she is—open to the merry winds and to the lusty sunshine's smiles—a cheerful, gay little metropolis that takes life for a blessing divine, and makes the most of God's bountiful gifts to man."

Centennial festivities in May appeared to involve the entire community. The cast alone for the "historic spectacular," Sandtrails to Contrails, "depicting the history and progress of Titusville, Florida," numbered several hundred, with four performances given at Draa Field. Early episodes depicted Seminoles—four dozen men, women, children, "Seminole Girl

Dancers" and a Seminole Princess Dancer, Charlotte Stud-still from the Studstill Dance Studio. The pageant director had elected to skip over the original settlers, the Ais tribe, which lived in the area centuries before "the white man," the show's point of reference. Episode XVII, "The Atomic Era," had one character: the atomic bomb, which, according to the program, played itself. Historic costuming seemed to persist all spring. Women sewed long skirts, aprons, and bonnets from the same Little House on the Prairie–type patterns; men appeared in white shirts, ribbon ties, and top hats. To one event, Mom lent a few antique gowns worn by her grandmother in Maine. If nothing else, it represented early snowbird garb. But if memory serves, neither she nor my father were involved in the festivities.

Titusville's historic homes were on display, notably Dummitt Castle, named for Captain Douglas Dummitt, who, sailing by the area around 1807, caught the heavy scent of wild orange blossoms and vowed to cultivate them. A decade later, he reappeared with budwood from Saint Augustine's Spanish oranges and planted trees on a land grant earned by fighting the Seminoles. Miraculously, it survived the Great Freeze of 1835, which killed other Florida groves to the ground; the rivers in Dummitt's proximity (Indian, Banana, Saint Johns) moderated temperatures. Thus the famous Indian River oranges—the sweetest ever, it's said—came to be, with other growers following Dummitt's lead. But the castle wasn't his. The Duke of Castellucio, who bought the grove after Dummitt's death, built the house as the Villa Castellucio, described by an architect friend as "an overreaching one-off example of a mid-19th century southern-Palladian cracker-influenced vernacular house . . . conveying Gothic-revival overtones."

It had been quite a sight, this wooden villa amid scrub and tall palmettos, backed to a mosquito-infested lagoon. Here, the duke and his duchess entertained visitors "from all over the world," leading one to wonder how those visitors got there, and why the duke and duchess exiled themselves in the first place. Eventually, the royal couple failed to entertain each other, partitioning their folly in half—a Jack-and-Jill estate. The home passed through several other hands, and when the government took the land, oranges and all, in 1964, the weathered antique was moved to a Titusville park, set up on blocks, and encircled by chain link and barbed wire. At the end of the centennial year, vandals burned it.

☾ ☾ ☾

In the fall of 1968, Titusville observed several firsts, such as the opening of an overdue walk-in psychiatric unit for troubled teenagers and adults. Families were stressed; some were coming apart; we knew one family in which the husband threatened his wife with a rifle dating back to the Korean War. On the positive side, more bikers were stopping by the Indian River seafood shacks for mullet, oysters, and grits, and citizens had access to six-channel cable TV. In November, between Apollo missions 7 and 8, the much-anticipated Miracle City Mall opened on US 1. By now, an Orlando advertising firm holding the state tourism account had divided Florida into "the twelve great regions of Florida," naming ours the Space Coast, after a nationwide study showed 40 percent of Americans wanted to visit the Apollo 11 moon launch. Bustling commerce was expected, despite a flattening national economy. Miracle City's dozens of stores, anchored by J. C. Penney and an improved Belk's, rivaled those in the older Searstown mall down the road. It even had a shop that sold paperback books. One day, reaching behind a display of Ian Flemings, I plucked out a single copy of Theodore Dreiser's *Sister Carrie*—my kind of miracle.

Because Titusville lacked sufficient retail for its growing size, most residents still relied on Orlando's stores, driving over on a Saturday with a long list. But the items I wanted, specific books and records, couldn't be found in the city, or required long afternoons of browsing without your parents around, so I ordered books by mail and joined the Columbia Record Club. I'd been "sending away" for years, starting with cereal box tops in exchange for plastic trinkets, advancing to the Frederick's of Hollywood catalog shown in *True Confessions*, and Chamber of Commerce brochures advertised in the back of *National Geographic*. I knew all about Tucson, Arizona, for example; once I'd shown interest, the city kept bugging me to retire there.

"Sending away" was cousin to searching for a clarinet teacher in another town. If what you needed wasn't available, just look elsewhere.

At least, that was a running theme in our family during the Titusville years. "Do not accept the limits of your immediate situation," I seemed to hear Mom say, although I'm not sure she ever uttered it out loud. And as my teens progressed, what I needed, besides music and lessons, was intangible: private space. There was no good place to practice; our little house was too cramped and hot. Although our single window unit chilled the living room well enough, the other members of my family constantly walked in from the carport, slamming the door or even switching on the TV, five feet away from my perch at the piano bench. Hiding out in my bedroom meant opening the windows and hosting a SWAT team of mosquitoes and Palmetto bugs, or rain from an afternoon downpour, noisy as crackling cellophane. Even worse were the bedroom's wholly unforgiving acoustics. Boxed in by concrete, sheetrock, and terrazzo flooring, I sounded to myself like a cheap kazoo, and if my new hormones pulsed full tilt, I burst out crying after one scale, in deep despair, boo-hooing because I'd never get any better, ever, and it wasn't fair, nothing was fair. I'd heard my parents, years before, murmur something about letting me skip a grade. Well, why hadn't they? As the months dragged on, my practice sessions grew more anxious and the diary entries more feverish. I needed lots of room, not just for my sound, but for my imagination, which leaped out of Titusville so often it seemed I'd already moved away. In the great tradition of alienated adolescents, I began to skip classes and drive around aimlessly.

I had to clear three hurdles to get away with skipping school, and I managed two of them before realizing I was setting myself up to break rules. The first was covering missed homework, which was easy, because I didn't have much. So deep was my passion for music, so sure was my goal to be a great clarinetist, that I had convinced the guidance counselor to let me demote myself from advanced classes to the regular kind. "I need to spend every free minute practicing," I explained to her, and after a mild protest, Miss Connor, who had a master's degree in conducting, praised my ambition and filled out the necessary forms.

The second hurdle was figuring out how to leave campus alone in a car without being questioned. School integration smoothed the way. After Titusville High and Gibson High combined, I worked as an assistant to the choral director, who'd been assigned Gibson's music room. Since part of my job was to transport music from one campus to the other, the parking lot monitors got used to seeing me load up the Falcon to make the hauls; they didn't realize the choral director had a free period during my work hour and never knew whether or not I showed up. Eventually, I started driving over the tracks, and away—toward the Indian River to watch the shore birds,

or into one of the orange groves north of town, where I might snitch a piece of fruit before returning to school.

One day I decided skipping one period wasn't enough—I needed at least two—and I developed the art of forging excuses. If you missed more than one class at Titusville High, you had to bring a note from home stating you were sick, or had a doctor's appointment. My mother had always written these, so I began faking notes from my father, whose hand no one knew. When I started skipping whole school days and afternoons as well, I had to explain to Mom and Dad why I wouldn't be home until five or six. That was easy. I was staying after school to practice my clarinet.

《 《 《

I didn't drive far at first, but nearly always headed north on
US Highway 1, past the Indian River and along the Atlantic
Ocean. The northern beach towns, I discovered, were poor relations to Palm Beach, Fort Lauderdale, and Miami, plagued by
land deals gone wrong, hotels not filled, lives changed for the
worse. Instead of golden, coarse-grained sand, they had fine gray
dirt. Instead of languorous coconut palms, they had scrub palmetto and wild, thigh-slicing grass. Most had no shells, no life-
guards, and no public showers. They were often deserted and
melancholy, even when the sun was shining. The only town of
any size along the 150-mile stretch between Titusville and the
state line at Jacksonville was Daytona Beach, which, outside of
spring break in March, contained nothing more than a handful of Indian River citrus shops and the ghosts of Henry Ford,
Louis Chevrolet, and Ransom Olds, who used to race their pro-
totypes in the sand.

New Smyrna Beach, thirty miles north of Titusville and
my favorite spot for writing poor-me poetry on the sand in
the rain, was settled in the mid-1700s by a Scottish physician,
Andrew Turnbull, who tried to create a Mediterranean colony by importing Greeks and Italians to labor on his plantation in exchange for plots of land. Turnbull's dream went bust,
but evidence of it remained: the ruins of a sugar mill, and Turnbull's unfinished house. There was also an Indian burial mound
nearby. I explored the sugar mill ruins several times, fingering
the cracks in the stones, creeping through empty doorways, but
I wouldn't leave the Falcon to examine the burial mound. All I
could see from my blue vinyl bench seat was a grassy hill, which
I imagined to be stuffed with bones.

If I'd driven beyond New Smyrna and Daytona Beach, I
might have seen the Fountain of Youth at Saint Augustine. But

one day, just north of Daytona, I turned inland on Florida 100, weaving through the poor farming and ranching villages of Andalusia and San Mateo. About ten miles past San Mateo, I caught US 17, which led me north along the Saint Johns River toward the small town of Green Cove Springs, where my first boyfriend, the only other clarinet player in the world as ambitious as I, lived.

Alone on the highway, I felt grown up and free, suspended in space. Time opened up, lengthened, spread for miles. No one knew where I was—no one could have found me. I rolled down the windows, let in the rain, even when it stormed hard enough to clear the buggy windshield. During this drive, and others, I began to identify an aversion to Titusville unrelated to the lack of high art: the presence of the Space Center itself, and its helium cry for progress. I had tried, on trips to Playalinda, to celebrate the launchpads down the beach, but never could. They were blights on a beautiful shore, symbols of land and lives warped or wiped out. It was sacrilege to say it, so I'd barely permitted myself to think it: the Space Center leaked anxiety and loss.

Along the Saint Johns, I found solace. Here, the magnolias bloomed as if filled with doves. Spanish moss drifted from grandfather oaks, glass-insulated telephone lines, the roofs of shanties and aluminum trailers. Small farms and fishing camps seemed to slide toward the water, as if to melt with it. Few outsiders had made fortunes here, no native ever dreamed of making one. Seminole Indians, I knew, once lived along the river, taking in runaway slaves from Georgia and South Carolina, and I was as likely to see a black farmer as a white one, plowing earth his family had squatted on several generations before. I passed fresh-laundered work shirts pinned to white string lines asway in the breeze, women in cotton dresses chasing tiny, biscuit-brown children who wore nothing but muddy underpants. The Saint Johns was the lower right-hand corner of the Deep South, a pocket of dank green beauty, and I, the transplant dreaming of escape to my rightful home in the north, craved the certain history of the potholed roads, the rusted-out signs, the country gas pumps, and the warm, beating heart of something.

Green Cove Springs had once been a popular spring-fed resort, its warm, sulfurous waters known for curing rheumatism "and a hundred complaints." Now, as far as I could tell, it was a Titusville without NASA: a sleepy river town that perked up on weekends for high school football. I had met my Green Cove friend in the only mixer I'd been part of: All-State band. Fat, redheaded, and excitable, Spence had stared at me obsessively during the first rehearsal, puffing his cheeks and crossing his eyes, trying to make me laugh. I don't know why he picked me to entertain, to crack up. I believed I looked serious and attentive and beyond such childishness, and maybe that was the point. A few months later we attended the same summer music camp and bonded over Vandoren reeds and alternate fingerings for high G.

When I got to Green Cove, I stopped at a pay phone and called the Clay County High School band room, where Spence spent the afternoons practicing and coaching younger students. I dropped my dime five times before working it into the slot. A girl with the voice of a small child whined hello. I could hear Spence in the background, yelling at someone to force more air through a saxophone, then yelling at the whiney girl for interrupting him. When he heard my voice, he screamed. I met him at the band room, and he paraded me around, announcing to everyone that I was even more talented than he was, "even though I beat her out at State." The kids seemed much younger than my Titusville classmates. The boys' haircuts were uneven and some of the girls had dirty ankles. I sped the 125 miles home in time for dinner.

Spence and I didn't last long. One week he finally declared his passion for me; the next week he announced he couldn't give me what I needed, whatever that meant. I'd wanted both proclamations, actually, and was relieved when they erupted back to back, for at home, I was beginning to feel ever more anxious and confused. The Falcon's muffler had disappeared—I couldn't admit it lay somewhere along the new interstate, so I fibbed it had fallen on the way to a Silvertones gig. I was preparing a concerto for a contest, the first solo I'd attempted with an accompaniment too difficult for Mom to pound out, and had to adjust to a new pianist, who was accurate, but bored with me, with the whole enterprise. And Miss Connor, the guidance counselor, was calling me in for college conferences because through some fluke of guesswork I had placed among the school's top ten scorers on the Florida twelfth grade test. I was sent to a meeting with the other nine, all straight-A students in calculus and biochemistry, courses I had never taken—indeed, my one go at the Science Fair had failed spectacularly when twenty-nine of the thirty dime-store mice undergoing my half-baked social experiments perished in the utility room during a hard freeze, and I was forced to fabricate the results, alongside the survivor racing desperately on its wheel. The judge, a local doctor, noted the even numbers on my graph, all divisible by four, and wondered where the other mice were. "I thought one was enough for display purposes," I said. Now in company with the scientists' kids, I squirmed as Mr. Everhart proclaimed us the leaders of tomorrow. Leafing through our school records, nodding proudly at each of us, he opened my folder, scanned my course load, frowned, and commented in front of everyone, that he didn't understand how I got there.

At the same time, my mother was applying herself to my activities with a new intensity; it began when her job at the VAB ended and she went to work in the hospital, which exactly corresponded with the start of the Silvertones and my high school years. Suddenly, she was buying volumes of popular hits for the two of us to play—far more fun than her old Red Cross military and Girl Scout songbooks—and accompanying other kids in the band. She was a reliable sight reader and good-natured partner to everyone, from the piccolo player to the baritone hornist. I was proud of her involvement until, to my horror, she began chaperoning band trips. Now she was riding up front in the Greyhound, standing every fifty miles or so to shush us. Only once, at a Panama City Beach motel, was I glad of her presence, when two sailors invited me and three other clarinet players to their room. We were flattered and stupid enough to go along with them, until a dark foreboding descended, and I announced, haughtily, "We can't stay. My mother is here."

V

In 1968, my grandfather died in Maine of heart failure. Losing him was a great sorrow. We hadn't the funds to fly to the funeral, so one of my mother's brothers loaned us the money. Mom suggested I bring my clarinet and play "Taps" at the end of the service. Surely she knew how tacky that would sound; her judgment must have been clouded by grief. I refused, sparing us embarrassment in the First Universalist Church, a classic New England house of worship with more references to Emerson than to Christ. Afterward, the family congregated at home, paying homage in the upstairs study, where, for decades, Grandfather had tied his own fishing flies. Cousins, six of us, examined the delicate bits of bird feathers and animal fur, the brass beads, the spools of waxed red, green, brown, and white thread, everything set out on a worktable, as if Grandfather had just stepped out for a cup of coffee. For once, Grandmother wasn't hovering, telling us what to do and how to do it, but accepting condolences in the parlor, in tears.

Mom still expressed a longing for Maine, planning our summer visits, sniffing out local Maine-iacs. She knew a Maine native at the cape who drove up every other week, burning up US 1 in less than twenty-four hours so he could stand on native soil for two days. Another Down Easter she named her estate executor. Her closest friend, Bertie Gillespie next door, was a Pennsylvania native who shared her outlook and temperament. I couldn't see it then, but Mom possessed no cohesive tribe in Titusville. Finding community was easier for families who had transferred together from the same NASA field office or aircraft manufacturing town in West Virginia, New Jersey, or California. Others met their kind at Saint Theresa's Catholic Church annual fair, where exotic foods like Polish sausage were cooked up by newcomers, assuaging homesickness and expanding Titusville's palate. Mom hung in. One last time, she made the newspaper, demonstrating Polynesian in-ground cooking, adapting the New England clambake for a semitropical audience.

Dad, to our surprise, mused about retiring someday to Indiana, though only one close relation, the sister who'd attended Purdue, remained. He was tired, our father, and, I understand now, somewhat depressed, though he'd summon his good humor for us, especially Mom, as on the afternoon he set his hand to our rangy shrubs, trimming and pruning every green, growing thing around the house. It was fall, and the Florida holly in the front yard was laden with bright red berries, the closest thing the state has to native Christmas foliage. Mom loved that bush, which had grown tall enough to qualify as a tree, and when she drove in from work and saw it reduced to a pole in the ground, she nearly wept.

"Mac!" she cried, "what did you do to the Florida holly?"

"I was just pruning, Helen. What's wrong?"

"It was at its peak, for Christmas!"

"I'm sorry," he grumbled. "I was just trying to get something done around here."

When I came home from school the next day, the Florida holly was right again, though a miracle didn't occur to me, as I pranced back to my room to pump out "In the Hall of the Mountain King." An hour later, Mom drove in and I heard her voice in the living room, high and soft with delight, and his, low and tender. The front door opened and shut, and I peeked out to see my parents admiring the Florida holly, its berried branches magnificently restored, like a story out of the Bible. Neighbors who had witnessed the holly's resurrection gathered on the sidewalk. Mom was radiant. "But how could this be, Mac?" she asked, and he led her closer to the tree to inspect his handiwork: a miraculous creation indeed, of cut branches and Scotch tape. The two of them, and the neighbors, burst out laughing. Oh, who could ever be mad at George?

《 《 《

In my senior year, Mom found yet another clarinet teacher: Richard Feasel, the clarinet professor at Stetson University, an hour away in Deland, and, as Harry Schmidt had, Dick Feasel pulled that old pedagogical trick: standing behind the student and sending his arms and hands forward of her waist to grasp and finger her clarinet, while she, arms down at her sides, merely blows through the mouthpiece. The point is to relieve the student of technical demands so she can focus on consistent air production, but from the student's point of view, it feels a bit like puppetry, or more, when the teacher's forearms nestle into her torso. This was no way to master the Hindemith sonata's mixed meters, and although I won a first at the state contest, the judge wrote, "If not for the flexibility of your pianist . . ."

Professor Feasel was the last straw. I'd leave Florida on the first bus, train, or plane. To a *Star-Advocate* reporter interviewing upcoming graduates, I brayed, "Of course, I will attend the Eastman School of Music in New York." But by spring, it was determined that, for financial reasons, I would attend a state-funded university, and I auditioned for and received scholarships for two. In May, Feasel pulled a surprise, offering me close to full funding to attend Stetson. I loathed the idea, but accepted his offer. My parents' situation weighed on me. There was some consolation: one or two members of the London Symphony, which had begun wintering in Daytona Beach, sometimes taught there. I confessed my disappointment to a new friend, Jesse, a French horn player in Spence's band who collected postcards of Renaissance art and aspired to a Catholic priesthood. We shared a love of poetry, exchanging favorites by Edna St. Vincent Millay, and together, complained bitterly about the lack of good taste and propriety about us. Although he was as desperate to leave small-town Florida as I was, Jesse gave me a deeply southern gift: his arm at the Green Cove prom, held in a plantation home. At evening's end, he kissed me in a field of warm cows.

(((

For graduation, I asked for and received a thesaurus. Over the years, my diary writing had spawned two published items: an imperious letter to the student newspaper, denouncing school spirit as the province of lost sheep, and a self-satisfied little piece for the *Star-Advocate*, which won a teen essay contest. "For me, mediocrity is monotony," I wrote, with a sniff—but when the essay appeared, I reddened, for seeing the thing in print brought home how priggish I sounded, and I was grateful when friends turned "mediocrity is monotony" into a laughable mantra, a joke on me. As a lighthearted memorial to my band career, Mom spray-painted my dirty white marching shoes silver, filled them with plastic lilacs, and mounted them on a gilded wood plaque from Grant's craft department. On both shoes, the leather toe box had rotted and split open from rain, mud, and my broad toes. After the drizzly ceremony at Draa Field, made bearable by the student seated next to me, a fellow named McBride whose back I'd stared at for seven years in alphabetically arranged classes, and who thought to bring an umbrella that day, Mom attempted a photograph in our backyard next to the orange tree, but I refused to pose proudly, instead lifting my gown high to show my thighs, or raising a middle finger and laughing. That evening, at Leslie's house, her father poured us each a celebratory gin and tonic so weak we could only pretend to inebriation. "We're drunk! We're drunk!" we crowed, two of the most naive, sheltered girls in the Class of '69.

☾ ☾ ☾

A month later, in the course of a weekend, the Titusville area's population swelled from forty thousand to several hundred thousand, as a great tide of people in cars, vans, campers, and boats poured into the county, filling motels, trailer parks, parking lots, and docks, and eventually road shoulders, median strips, river islands, and riverbanks. The Apollo 11 launch, set for the morning of Tuesday, July 15, had drawn visitors from all over the world, transforming Titusville and the other Space

Coast communities into something resembling Woodstock, a
month hence. Right in town, the Indian River offered a clear
view of the Vehicle Assembly Building and the launch pad holding a Saturn V destined for the moon, with the first man to
walk on the lunar surface.

No matter how badly members of my class might have
wanted to move on, get out of Dodge, many were still in town,
and some I contacted later vividly remembered the scene, apro-
pos of seventeen- and eighteen-year-olds.

Mike Dent had been close to launch preparations for weeks,
having landed a summer job at the cape working for Bendix and
the Apollo program. With top security clearance, he clocked in
every day at the Operations and Checkout Building, equipped
with pocket protector, snap-on tie, and slide ruler. "I made an
incredible four hundred dollars a week," he said.

"My job was to prepare the coversheet snapshot of the
30-day, 24-hour schedule for the Apollo 11, 12, and 13
launches. The actual scheduling took maybe an hour from start
to finish. I had a large board with magnetic bars. I put together
the chart, called a photographer who snapped a shot, and all
the engineers, astronauts, and managers would receive it the
next day. I produced a countdown of all operations including
the Apollo 11 moon launch! I had access to a company car and
a walky-talky and several times had to go off location to coor-
dinate the opening of the large bay doors to the OCB. It would
take up to 20 minutes to open them and if the 'Super-Guppy'
flew in from California with a command module or stage, I
would radio in to the 'doorman' that the plane had landed, and
estimate how long it would be before it arrived at the building. It was exciting to be part of this moment in time. I even ate
lunch with the astronauts."

The night before the launch, Titusville streets boiled with activity. Rick Roberts, whose father, a builder who had moved his family to Titusville in 1956, spent the evening driving around town in his Datsun 2000 roadster with a friend, "checking out all the tourist girls."

"We had the top down and were having the time of our lives. Neither one of us was totally aware history was about to be made—to us it was like a circus or carnival event. We rode along the waterfront looking out over the Indian River and the launch pad all lit up. The lights reflecting off the water. It seemed to last forever."

Jan Ewen Grimard, whose parents owned Electronic Sound and Nova TV, took advantage of the tourist trade: "My mother, being very artsy and crafty, made earrings from seashells that I thought were too big and gaudy and sent me down to the river to sell them. I walked around meeting all kinds of people and what a shock—those earrings sold like crazy!"

That night, as we teens strolled the riverbank, the fishing pier, the causeway bridge, the shrimp shacks and fast food joints on US 1, we encountered hippies with guitars crooning "Puff the Magic Dragon," sorority sisters in matching Greek letter t-shirts, ex-military waving American flags, and all manner of official and unofficial groups. We noticed every English language accent we thought possible, and other tongues: German, French, Spanish, Norwegian. Pat West Marovich, whose father worked for TWA and Boeing, remembered how exciting it was, "talking to people from all over the world." Angela Lynch echoed the memory of "walking up and down the river, meeting hundreds of people, sharing stories, playing games, and singing."

"Every inch of the highway was filled," she said. "We owned US 1!"

All night, the sky rang with laughter, shouts, singing,

whoops, and occasionally, a reverberating stillness. I camped on the river with a friend's family. At dawn, I awoke on a blanket in the sand and smelled fried bacon and eggs from the camper next to our tent, heard the occupants, a retired couple from Ohio, preparing to record the launch with tape recorder, video camera, and still camera. Their radio and portable television crackled with simultaneous launch updates. It suddenly occurred to me that neither of these wayfarers would witness the moon shoot with a naked eye or ear.

As the sun rose, the riverbank came alive once more, a dawn chorus of human voices low, high, dense, airy, muddy, articulated. Sounds of beverage can pop-tops, giggling toddlers, more guitar, "Michael Row the Boat Ashore." Water sloshing against the ribbed strand. Gulls' desperate, two-syllable cries, pelicans' abrupt squawks, great herons' burred yawp. The sky: mauve, peach, yellow, chromium blue. A few clouds up high, above the Saturn V, incised, to our eyes, as sharply against the green-silver landscape as the torch on a dime.

In the US 1 restaurants, some of my classmates were busy feeding the crowds. Tom Hill worked at the Holiday Inn on the Indian River as "a utilities worker: dishwasher, pots and pans, mop."

"The lines to eat and use the bathroom were amazingly long," he said. "The only way to feed the masses was to do a buffet with just scrambled eggs, bacon, sausage, and toast. The next thing was to supply enough plates, silverware, and cups. That was me, putting the plates, silverware, and cups in the dishwashing machine as fast as possible. I have never worked that hard in my life."

Jo Lynn Johnson Jorczak also worked that morning, as a waitress at Walgreen's Restaurant in Miracle City Mall. "I had been lucky to get this job for the summer, earning $1.00 an hour plus tips!" she told me. "I was headed to college in the fall and the extra money would help with expenses.

"The restaurant opened much earlier than normal. The booths and the stools at the counter quickly filled, and the first thing to go was the blood-of-life machine, COFFEE. We could not brew it fast enough to satisfy the customers.

"Eventually, out of frustration, a few of the waitresses, myself included, crossed our arms and refused to take one more order until things caught up. Our manager was not too happy, threatening to fire us if we didn't get back to work, but we all knew he was as frustrated as we were and that he would not follow through on his threat, or so we hoped!

"Finally, and almost as quietly as lifting fog, people began to drift out and there were no new customers. Launch time was getting close. As the last customer scurried out, the manager locked the entry to the mall and we went outside to join hundreds and hundreds of people, standing in the parking lot."

Two classmates viewed the launch from rooftops. Bob Kemp, whose family had been in town just two years, was working launch day at Spangler lumberyard, "trying to scrape up a few bucks for school in the fall.

"Titusville was packed with onlookers. Business came to a standstill, as did local traffic. So we all climbed up to Spangler's roof to watch it go."

Ed Wirth, who had fallen ill earlier that summer, was in Jess Parrish Hospital preparing to be discharged. But he was positioned better than any of us, atop the new seven-story building with the doctors and nurses. "We probably had the most uncrowded view of the shot," he said.

And one classmate got so close to the astronauts that morning he might have shaken hands with them. John Kadlec worked in the Space Center's industrial area for Federal Electric,

the company his father also worked for. That morning, Kadlecs
senior and junior left early for their jobs, unsure how long it
would take. "US 1 was a parking lot," John said. "Fortunately,
they'd opened the new NASA causeway so cape workers could
get in. Since we were over an hour early, Dad decided to drive
past the MSOB (Manned Space Operations Building) because
we saw a lot of activity over there. We parked and walked over
to where dozens of people, camera crews, etcetera. were gathered. I elbowed my way to the rope line. After a few minutes,
the crew of Apollo 11 walked out of the building in their space
suits, carrying their air conditioners. They walked right at me,
then turned left and walked to the van that carried them to the
launch pad. Here I was, a seventeen-year-old kid, watching Neil
Armstrong, Buzz Aldrin, and Michael Collins walk within ten
feet of me, literally on their way to the moon. It is a memory I
will never forget."

On the riverbank with my friend and her family, I washed
down a couple of Krispy Kremes with coffee, made conversation

with visitors in the surrounding crowd, offering local authority. Sure, I knew people who worked out there—I knew people
out there right now, and my friend knew one in the VIP view-
ing stands! Oh yes, we had been here all along, since the beginning, in on the ground floor, part of the great push toward this
very morning, the very moment coming up, yes, we were all so
proud, and I was, too, I meant it, I did, something broke open
right then, I meant it, I wouldn't have missed it.

Now our transistor radio was tuned to the launch broadcast,
and the voice of Mission Control, marking the slow minutes
toward official countdown. A little after 9:00 a.m., we began to
situate ourselves just so for a clear view, wondering if that tall
guy was going to stand and block the way, if two feet to the left
meant obstruction by cabbage palm—as if anyone, really, could
miss a 363-foot, 6,698,746-pound rocket ignite, blow a pounding, muscular cloud of smoke and in an agonizing thrust, ele-
vate past its monstrous, crane-like supports, and actually keep
moving up and up, levitating, gathering, lifting and lifting
higher, higher, until the impossible mission—after all, after
everything given and lost and yet given again—was inevitable.

A minute to go, and counting. Excited chatter subsided. Even
the gulls. The illusion of stillness. Everyone held their breath,
stared across the river, shielding their eyes against the sun. Only
the slightest movements: shifting of feet, smoothing of hair,
adjustment of glasses. Tears, already.

And the voice of Mission Control:

T-minus fifteen seconds and counting
  Guidance is internal
  Twelve
  Eleven
  Ten

Nine
Ignition sequence starts
Six
Five
Four
Three
Two
One
Zero
All engines running
Lift-off, we have a lift-off,
32 minutes past the hour,
Lift-off on Apollo 11
Tower cleared—

We followed it, up and up, our faces lit and lifted by that thundering detonation, the fiery detachment, the coil of smoke, and the majestic ascent of an invention jammed with other inventions, yet appearing, as it pulled away from us and sought the higher blue, to be no more than a silver fish, and finally, a blinking star. We were with it, we were right up there, gasping, roaring, and then we were standing on the ground, exhaling, shaking our heads, as along the wild riverbank thickets of scarlet Turk's-cap quivered, magnolia leaves loosened and sank to the grass, mockingbirds fluttered and returned to their perches, conforming shoulders and wings.

For one sweet, extended moment, it occluded everything else in the world.

❨ ❨ ❨

Four afternoons later, the lunar module *Eagle* touched down in the Sea of Tranquility, tapping the moon's surface, stirring its dreadful silence. Every television set, even my family's dusty old Westinghouse, was tuned in for astronauts Armstrong and Aldrin's Moon to Earth broadcast.

In Titusville, Joan Hare Massey, whose father had been an engineer with the space program since the 1950s, watched with friends, "scared that when the astronauts took the first step out of the capsule onto the moon's surface it would just swallow them up in lunar dust." Greg High, whose step-grandfather cleared jungle for five launch pads, was in class at Brevard Junior College. "There was much ado about Armstrong's words. Neil Armstrong says he said, "That's one small step for *a* man . . . one giant leap for mankind." But what we all heard was "That's one small step for man, one giant leap for mankind. There was a blip in the transmission."

Jay Carothers's father had worked on the Apollo 11 mission, but had left town weeks before the launch to attend the United States Naval Academy in Annapolis. "After running and marching all day, the upper classmen called me in and let me sit up front near the TV for the moon broadcast, since they knew my father had worked on that mission. It gave me a boost. . . if the astronauts could make it to the moon, I could make it through my plebe year."

(((

Some classmates had left the area well before the launch, their parents laid off or reassigned. Gerald Wayne Stephenson's father was the prime contractor for heating and ventilation systems in the VAB and the launch control building complex.

"In February, my father told us we were moving to Dalton, Georgia, for that was where the money was to be made. I couldn't understand how we were useless to NASA but knew everything that needed to be built for the space program was completed. I felt proud watching the First Steps on the moon, and remember going out at night, looking up at the sky and crying, with pride, yes, and hurt, because I wasn't where it started on the ground."

Mark Kimmell considers himself a member of the class even though his family moved to Santa Monica at the end of 1967. His father had worked at the cape since 1958. The summer of 1969, he held a job as far from modern technology as one could imagine.

"I was working with my uncle in the wheat harvest. We were in a remote area of South Dakota during the time of the launch and landing. The nearest evidence of civilization, a crossroads store and gas station, was about 35 miles away. There was nothing but pastureland and wheat fields to the horizon in every direction.

"These few days' harvest represented a big percentage of the year's income for the farmers we worked for. The fact that there was a missile launch in Florida, even one holding the possibility of landing a man on the moon, was of little interest to them. I got what news coverage I could by listening to a transistor radio from the wheat field. I was excited to look up at the moon and know one of our astronauts was standing there, but my feelings were my own and not shared by the farmers, or other guys on the harvest crew."

And Mike Dent, the classmate who'd eaten lunch with the astronauts, recalls the moon telecast, as well as a less exciting aftermath.

"One day soon after the launch, a pink slip was in my paycheck. While Neil Armstrong was walking on the moon, the printing presses were issuing these. Not just me, but lots of people felt the immediate hatchet. At the peak of America's space program, it was dismantled. It was sad."

❮ ❮ ❮

A few weeks later, more than two-thirds of us entered college, a large proportion, then, for a public high school, our stories radiating from NASA's fishbowl. Others enlisted in the armed forces and went to Vietnam, our generation's war. The national quest for superiority we'd internalized, perhaps personally employed, had come to a kind of fruition, and even though the Apollo program continued through 1972, it had settled out, as had Titusville, which stopped growing. We were on our own, now, living into another future.

I attended Stetson to study with Mr. Feasel, the teacher who'd tried the arms-around-the-middle technique. The school, whose social life prided all-white sororities, fraternities, and a Baptist Student Center, lacked the wider cultural opportunities of a large university, and I was miserable. At the end of the year I, and two equally disenchanted friends, transferred to Florida State in Tallahassee, a better fit for us, though, in my private lessons, I had to endure Harry Schmidt's ridiculous Positioner, sexist jokes, and dismissal of my ambition—there were no alternatives, then, no forums for young women's complaints. But I practiced and studied hard in spite of it and enjoyed my years at FSU, working part-time jobs and applying for National Defense Student Loans, offspring of the Cold War's National Defense Education Act. Sputnik had inadvertently funded my lessons on Debussy's *Première Rhapsodie*, though every spring, that critical support was threatened and Mom and Dad sweated anew over the required forms, or whether there would be any forms at all.

The summer before my final semester, Dad offered Mom, Estalene, and me one last family vacation in Maine. It was not pleasant. At twenty and twenty-two, my sister and I were past a historic reenactment of childhood car trips, but worse, Dad was on edge the whole time, his temper short, his patience shattering over the smallest disputes, like when to stop for lunch or the bathroom. Why, I wondered, had he insisted on this three-thousand-mile round-trip journey? At the end of it I complained to Mom, who whispered something about prostate trouble, but I didn't understand what that meant to a man driving an old Ford the entire length of the Atlantic seaboard. In September, my father, the closet poet, sent me the longest letter of my college years, explaining himself with a prescience that still haunts me.

> Dear Ann,
>
> Don't worry (and tell Estalene not to worry) about federal funds cut-off whether temporary or permanent. We will see it through financially one way or another. The most important thing you can do (both of you) is to continue excellent grades. *When not endangering good grades*, any income you can earn, but that comes second.
>
> The vacation was wonderful, we thought, and hope you girls enjoyed it as much as we did. The only fly in the ointment for me was the discomfort and sometimes a bit of pain I experienced which made me "grumpy" at times. I knew the trip would aggravate my "ailment," but I so wanted Mom and you girls to have a Maine vacation, also me of course, that I was anxious to take advantage of what might be our last chance for such a nice long time together; for who knows what the future holds. I'm not pessimistic in the forgoing, just facing the inevitable change of things as we go through life.
>
> Much love to you and Estalene,
> Dad

With Dad's reassurance, my last year in Tallahassee flew by, and I finally made it north, to Michigan, eagerly offering a net bag of Indian River oranges to my new major professor, a warm, avuncular man who had played with the Marine Band. "Well, well," he said, accepting the fruit, "It's been a long time since I had a student from the South."

Down to Earth

The campus police notified me on November 2—All Soul's Day, I learned later, having attended mostly Methodist churches, which observed few liturgical holidays outside Christmas and Easter. Now there would be a new holiday to observe, a day to remember, that November 2 and every one after that, the day in 1974 when an officer from the University of Michigan's security force rapped on the door of my dorm room, asked was I who I was. Then, "Call your aunt in Maine, immediately. Your parents have been in an accident."

Accident stands erect at the edge of a shelf, falls off, breaks. It is a given, it is a done deal. You taste the metal of inevitability, you hear the dull thump of something large, lost.

Your mother and father were on a trip. Take the next flight to Orlando. Your neighbors will meet you and take you to the hospital.

Hospital is pity so delicate you know you're in for heartsplitting news, biting astringents applied with the softest of cloths. My heart is not in my throat, it has jumped up into my jaws, which knock back and forth on clay hinges as I sleepwalk through the act of asking a friend, Can you take me, Detroit Metro, a flight at eleven, I'll pack fast.

The long flight, the long stares out the window. Typically intense graduate music student, trying inexplicably to read Kierkegaard and checking her nose periodically for shine (it was something to do).

I chew the airline chicken, try to make Kierkegaard relate to the moment. I nearly succeed. Or does the convoluted theology I barely understand merely keep my imagination on hold? I know nothing except Accident. And it will be hours before this word reveals the story behind it. Now it is dusk, the plane lands near orange trees, our next-door neighbors, the Gillespies, greet me at the gate, tell me we are going straight to a hospital near the Space Center. The accident happened yesterday, Bertie and Bill whisper. Your folks were on their way to see friends in Tampa. I nod, too frightened to press for details. I ask only if the hospital has good doctors. "They are receiving excellent care," Bertie says. I pick at my cuticles, hiding my hands in the well of my skirt. Bill asks me about school and I force some meaningless sentences about my impatience with Heinrich Schenker's theory of harmony. The drive takes forty-five minutes. It is eighty degrees out, and I shiver the whole way.

Bertie guides me down the green corridor. Let's stop by the chapel first, she says, and I suspect nothing more than a moment of prayer, for Bertie would do that, but we step inside and I am in the midst of what, in any other room, would appear to be a birthday surprise party, but it is not, it is a crowd of people, some I do not recognize, all from Titusville First Methodist, all waiting to surround me, and they do, as my sister moves from their midst to tell me, Oh, Ann, Dad went four hours ago.

My mother is completely white. She is nearly six feet long, commands her intensive care bed as once, with her poised and confident stride, she commanded the eyes of strangers in a room. Now I am a stranger, gazing in shock at her thoroughly blanketed form, none of her flesh showing except for the pale skin of her face below the skull, taped soundly like a cut thumb. The nurse tells me the surgeon shaved her rich black and silver hair to drain fluid from her brain. Next to the bed, the square eye of a machine flickers red with my mother's serrated pulse. I feel the nurse watching for my reaction, preparing to catch me if I faint. My mother is completely white, she is sleeping, she is dreaming, she is wrapped in ancient, magical gauze and will rise

up from the bed, shake off the tubes and wires, and float some-
place where she will look down kindly and tell me that it is all
right, it is a dream, I will wake up.

⟨ ⟨ ⟨

We slept in our old bedrooms in the tiny tract house, awash in
our parents' scents. Our bodies ached from an excess of sorrow, sobs that, with no warning, ruptured our chests. Here were
our father's blue cotton pajamas, still hanging on the back of
the bathroom door. His body, stopped just short of sixty-eight
years, was at the funeral home, waiting. Waiting for our mother's fifty-seven-year-old one, because, said the surgeon, she was
holding on by a very fine thread, and we should wait a few days
because—no one actually articulated this—one double funeral
would be easier to orchestrate than two single ones. If our
mother continued to live, she would never awaken. I prayed for
her death.

One of my mother's brothers, a biologist for the state of
Maine, flew down to help us. My father's sisters and brothers,
older people in their seventies, drove straight through from Indiana, stopping only to change drivers. Neighbors brought food.
The minister visited daily. Mid-week, the surgeon phoned and
said there were only a few hours left. Estalene, our uncle, and I
drove over then, but we were too late. They had already turned
off the machines. Estalene stepped forward to touch one of our
mother's blanketed feet. I hung back to watch and remember
the scene.

Someone asked me to plan the funeral music. For an opening
hymn, I chose Luther's "A Mighty Fortress," not imagining how
many citizens would pack First Methodist that day, the massed
voices somehow transforming a declaration of faith into a lam-
entation. I was stunned. Had the crowd come to support my sis-

ter and me? Were some here out of curiosity, or had my parents really affected that many people? I was five years gone from the town, now, and when I lived there, I was so self-consumed I'd missed or ignored the parts of my parents' lives that didn't directly involve me. I had taken them for granted, and the crowd at Titusville First Methodist was a measure of how much. The minister offered two official resolutions, acknowledging their contributions to church and community life, such as my father's work on committees, and my mother's with youth, mentoring teens at a church coffee house my sister helped start. I'd forgotten all about it. Now, the pain of losing them multiplied, a rippling mosaic of grief and regret. And alongside it, a great wave of received love, comforting and distressing, too, for it dissolved my little house of separateness.

My sister and I found it difficult to decide where Mom and Dad should be buried. Not Titusville, of course not. They—we—weren't from there. Maine or Indiana, then. When an aunt offered a plot in Bluegrass Cemetery, we accepted it, relieved of the choice, returning Dad to the place he once couldn't wait to leave, not returning Mom to the place she'd missed, and where Haverill, their firstborn, was buried. It has bothered me ever since.

Titusville, FL
November 8, 2011
Last night's dream:

I was being coaxed into a weekend car trip, one that would entail more time driving than relaxing at the destination. A man and two children, a boy and a girl, were egging me on. I wasn't sure how I was connected to these people. No, I didn't think it was a good idea. We'd no sooner arrive than we'd have to return! And I hadn't packed.

You don't need anything, the children cried, just the clothes on your back! I thought, maybe they're right. Who needs anything else for such a trip? But I returned to a house to get a few things. I was frightened, because someone had once robbed me in that house and I was scared to go there. I was afraid I'd be locked out, further proof of the thoroughness of the robbery. The man, the father of the children, went with me to the house, to help me break in. However, when I tried the front door myself, it opened easily! There, sleeping on the mat just inside the door was my beloved dog Jake, who I'd given up in a previous life. But it doesn't look like Jake, I said. He's older. It is Jake, said the man, who now seemed older, too.

Jake recognized me, got up, wagging his tail, came to be petted, like always. I burst into tears. Jake, returned to me! Now I was afraid that the robber, who'd stolen Jake, and other things, and locked me out of my house, was still inside. Looking beyond Jake, down the center hallway, I thought I saw a larger man, a friendly one, walking toward me, his arms outstretched.

But the dream stopped there, because I was sobbing, weeping, for real, and woke myself up. Jake returned to me! Dear, dear Jake!

((((((

Thirty-eight years have passed since I lost them. More than half my life, now. Still, I occasionally hear their measured footsteps down the hall, their voices mingling with purpose in the next room, as if one of them might soon tap my door and remind me the school bus is here, or dinner's ready, or it's time to get dressed for church. And since I'm now about the same age they were when they died, they've begun appearing in my mirror as

I've grown into a blend of both, with her classic oval face and oxbow cheekbones, his heavy-lidded brown eyes, tan skin, and prominent nose. Sometimes I unpack what turned out to be their last picture, taken by Bertie or Bill a few months before the accident, and hold it up to the glass and compare, make sure. Yes, here we are, possessed of our family's gaze, thoughtful, a little reserved, they, utterly still in a Florida backyard moment, reminding me who and where I'm from; I, moving into my sixties in Texas, bending closer toward their reflections, confessing my desire to free their images, animate them in a way that seems true, before I, too, fail to draw breath.

《 《 《

When I was growing up in Titusville, I heard our postman, a Mims native, refer mournfully to "The Old Florida," as if a dear old biddy named Florida had long ago passed to the other side, a withered hibiscus behind one ear, dragging the state's glory behind her like a soggy scarf. If you paid attention, you might sight evidence of Old Florida: in a slice of wild ocean caught between two condos, a Cracker-made fishing lure at a flea market, an abandoned roadside picnic area, its concrete shelters swathed in kudzu. Years later, I uncovered that cult of newspapermen who wrote elegant hymns to cane-pole fishing in slow rivers, falling-down camps their fathers built, backcountry characters held together by strong women, tobacco, and homemade hooch. "We knew the REAL Florida," they said, shaking their collective heads, "and it's all gone. The rest of you will never know." I wondered what age must one become, to take the old-timer's stance without pretension or embarrassment. I wondered if this stance was limited to men.

Someone once wrote that New Englanders and Southerners are the most elegiac Americans. Perhaps the east holds more

"American" history? Never mind, let somebody else study the question. I'm drawn to the elegiac because it gathers life into a blessed fullness. It offers an arc, beginning to end, a satisfying completion, like a rainbow after a storm in the Atlantic. As an elegist, I can also take on a well of both joy and sadness, in remembrance. Just so, a totality of feeling may fill me and pour itself out in tears or sobs or a long run or a thorough cleaning of the house, forcing me to drop down to the couch or the floor, spent, wasted, consummated.

"There," I say, happy with exhaustion. "That is all. All!"

And the well begins to fill again.

((((((

During that month in the Titusville bungalow, I drove up US 1, my old school-skipping route, a number of times, even as far as Daytona Beach, to a Barnes & Noble, the closest large bookstore. Titusville still doesn't have one, unless you count the

Book Rack, a hole-in-the-wall crammed with secondhand mysteries and romance novels. I'd dropped into the Book Rack early on, and, in a replay of *Sister Carrie*'s appearance at Miracle City, discovered a copy of Jean Cocteau's *Les enfants terribles* in a pile of Danielle Steels, and rescued it.

North of town, between Mims and the village of Scottsmoor, I noticed a series of small, low signs on the highway shoulder, reminding drivers that Butrico Groves, a name I remembered, was just one mile, half a mile, quarter mile ahead, TURN HERE. Since it was the only grove advertised, possibly the only grove left, I thought I'd better obey. A few blocks deep into a rural neighborhood, a right-hand turn on Seminole Street, and there was a grove and an open barn, with wide bins of fresh-picked oranges and grapefruit for sale. The owner, a burly fellow, hailed me with gusto and invited Cole to romp with his golden retriever, while he told me his story. He was relatively new to Florida, he said, having come down with his wife from Virginia one recent winter to escape the cold and take in the Gator Bowl. In their ramblings, the pair discovered the grove's original owner was retiring after fifty years, and made a quick decision to buy it. They quit their high-revs jobs in Virginia, sold their house, and headed back down. In three days, they learned to pick, pack, and ship fruit.

It was the opportunity of a lifetime.

As far as I could tell, the grove was doing well, not from local business but from shipping gift boxes north, though the man's wife, I noted, worked at Jess Parrish Hospital. When I said I used to be a local, the owner offered me a half bushel of fruit, my choice, insisting I sample each variety first. As I stood there, biting into, chewing, slurping up one orange slice after another, rinsing my fingers under an antique spigot, it occurred to me I was still pretty good at the art of holding the fruit slightly away from the body and bending toward and over it, so as not to drip juice on my clothing or chin.

Butrico's was not far from the northernmost end of Kennedy Parkway, or Highway 3, which runs down through Merritt Island National Wildlife Refuge and Canaveral National Seashore property, so I left US 1 and doubled back to Titusville via 3, curious to see if anything was left of the towns sacrificed for the space program. There was very little. A bit of chewed-up asphalt road here, an overgrown dirt driveway there. Anything built to stand vertical had been razed, agricultural communities like Shiloh and Allenhurst become less than ghost towns. Clifton, founded by a former slave, is marked by a state historical sign for the Clifton Colored School, 1890–91, one of the first schools for black children in Brevard County. Here, I stopped for a look and a brief hike back of the sign. But nothing remained of the school, except that left to the imagination.

Farther down the road, I pulled over to the Fish and Wildlife Service's Manatee View Observation Deck, new since my time, along Haulover Canal, the waterway connecting Mosquito Lagoon and the Indian River. Here, visitors can observe friendly thousand-pound vegetarians munching submerged plants, or gamboling about in the canal, with no obstructions, except for an occasional slow boat passing through.

But if the mammals seem free of predators, they are not. Something in the Indian River estuary is killing them off, I learned. All signs point to insidious ground and water pollution from lawn fertilizer and the thousands of septic tanks Titusville and other Space Coast towns installed en masse during the roaring '60s. Nitrogen levels have spiked, spawning algae and killing rich beds of seagrass, both a staple of the manatee's diet and a breeding ground for fish, which are a staple of the pelican's diet. And on and on. Apparently leaving Earth required ruining part of it. But no one paid attention to that, then.

(((

A few mornings after the drive down Highway 3, I rose very early and drove out to Playalinda to watch the sun come up. Since quitting Titusville, I'd seen spectacular sunrises from wild coasts in places like Maine, Hawaii, and Costa Rica, and wondered if my hometown beach would still impress. On this trip, instead of resenting the long drive, I enjoyed the time it took, finding comfort in the long views of marsh and scrub unfolding toward the ocean, a delicious, languid stretch, not an imposition. When I arrived, the parking lot was deserted; I'd even beat the usual handful of weekend fishermen. Climbing the wooden walkway over the dunes, I shivered a little in my windbreaker, pleased to be awakened so. I descended to the shore, spread a towel, opened a thermos of strong coffee, and dug my toes into the sand, to wait. At water's edge, sandpipers skittered back and forth, pecking at invisible sustenance.

Large violet clouds lay on the horizon, flounced high, shifting, shredding in spots like wet tissue, fugitive curtains. The whole was backlit by the waiting star, its fire striking first the clumped edges. The gilding deepened, and the sky above shaded from charcoal to pale yellow to pumpkin. The sun broke through the top of the heaped clouds, and as it lifted free of them, everything else on the horizon fell back, leaving the sun suspended in a smoky blue sky, casting a long, glittering streak across the water that ran to the shore, to the cool, bare soles of my feet.

In that moment, it was the only sunrise, it was all sunrises. It did not matter where I was, who or what town had sent me here. I heard no composed music, only splashing water and piping birds.

In a while, I turned slightly to the right, catching sight of three lit service towers in the NASA complex. I'd glimpsed them earlier, had felt their presence. Up rose that old ambivalence, the aversion that had bothered me so when I was young. I still didn't know what to make of it. I shrugged and stood to walk the shore, in the opposite direction.

(((

A few nights later, I signed on for a night kayak trip in Mosquito Lagoon. The kayaking company's founder was Laurilee Thompson, a classmate whose grandparents had been evicted from Merritt Island. Her father was a well-known boatbuilder. The kayak company was a move toward ecotourism, the granddaughter eager to share what remains, or has been preserved, and to help refresh Titusville's post-Apollo economy. In high school, Laurilee had done me one better in class-skipping, keeping a rowboat tied by the riverbank across from THS, leaving campus when she wanted, paddling to an island where no one could find her. School authorities couldn't have checked in with her parents, either. She'd given Burger King's pay phone as her home number. I thought it fitting, when Laurilee offered to accompany me on the kayak trip.

We met at dusk in a parking lot near the causeway and took her pickup out State Road 406 over the Indian River, turning left on Kennedy Parkway by Dummitt Cove and hanging another quick left toward the Haulover Canal boat launch. A few trucks and cars were parked toward the end by the water, and two vans with kayak cargo hove into view. We got out, soaked our skin and clothes with insect repellant, and surveyed the lagoon. Just beyond, we saw scraps of land that make up Klondike Beach, linking Apollo Beach to the north and Playalinda to the south. As we pulled on our life jackets, we spoke with others waiting to push off, among them two women, former classmates who still lived in the area. They'd kayaked here before and raved about the night trip. They also told me how two other classmates had, in the 1970s, been busted for selling fake moon rocks to tourists. I realized that by leaving for a long time, I had missed both an outdoor adventure and some darned good sequels.

After my folks died, I set aside my seven years in Titusville. My life started over when I was entirely on my own, severed, it seemed, from my past, living in a markedly different way from anything I'd expected. Occasionally, I felt a certain freedom, a release from my previous existence, like a balloon let go suddenly, helium lifting the fragile sphere up and up. But I can't describe that free feeling as a rebirth; the flight was often precarious, the balloon responding too readily to the weather around it. Eventually the helium spent itself and the balloon touched the ground and began to take on weight.

And the thought struck me: how tempting it could be, once one has left the scene of his or her youth, to mark it out in extremes, to manufacture a neat autobiography. The hometown was either heaven or hell, classmates friendly or snobbish. The old place was sacred ground that "made you what you are today" or you couldn't possibly have lived in this dump. Either way, you freeze the town and its people in that time, or deform them to suit the way you see yourself now. As if life isn't fluid.

Now, Laurilee and our classmates were calf-deep in the water, drudging in the briny muck, lowering our bottoms into single kayaks and pushing off with our paddles. I was grateful

for a good grip this evening. The hand ailment that had forced
my clarinet into premature retirement many years before had
not flared up this day. Overhead, the sky was nearly dark, and
cloudless, holding a half moon and speckled with soft, blinking
stars. Because Laurilee knew the lagoon like a neighborhood, we
were allowed to explore apart from the larger group, and we four
headed east, out toward Klondike Beach and the Atlantic, then
northwest into a smattering of low, marshy islands. As Laurilee led us close to a mangrove islet, she instructed us to whap
the lagoon's surface near the visible stilt roots, to splash it, and
as we did, great spirals of thick, glowing water leaped before us,
as if the lagoon were a creature, its bright arms reaching up out
of the depths. But there was more than one creature. We were,
she said, watching millions of dinoflagellates—photosynthetic
microplankton—springing around us, having absorbed light all
day. Why they fire in reaction to water pressure is not known for
certain, but it's thought the glow is a defense against predators;
it disorients intruders or attracts lower-strata predators to manage threats at the top.

Microplankton light up because they think they're about to
be eaten.

And just beyond us, in the near distance, stood the same
brilliant service towers I'd turned away from earlier, and more
lights, lower to the ground, made visible by the night sky. For a
moment, all were part of a natural tableau, compelled to glow
heavenward.

I could not look away from the towers now, for though I
decried the powers and circumstances that demanded them,
their hideous blight on the landscape, the anxiety and loss they
still leaked, I understood the individual compulsions they represented, as I understood my own compulsion to make music
and write, and realized I shared common ground with the thou-

sands of men and women who together had made and managed the towers and rockets, who held their jobs or callings dear. For before a nation's war cry came a great, ennobling aspiration: to accomplish what seemed impossible, to exceed the limits of life on Earth—and that spirit had alit in me, too. I remembered an Apollo scrapbook assembled by a classmate's mother, for her husband: "from one person who knows what you really did for the space program—metaphysically that is—and is very, very proud of you." For some, the effort had transcended competition, war, profits. It had been life's sacred work, its inexplicable reach, as music and language have been mine.

Again, I turned my face upward to encompass the half moon, and the stars above us, shining with light generated, I knew, from intense inner pressure. Hot lights above, hot lights below. And in between, a great space to "conquer," as the old slogans would have it, but not conquerable. The word can't reasonably apply to the unknown. The unknown, I think, is not an enemy to be fought, but a great mystery to be allowed, respected, and explored with care. In the allowing, secrets might be revealed, knowledge approached, memories transformed.

⟨ ⟨ ⟨

One warm spring morning in 1982, ten years after the Apollo missions were completed, a real estate developer in Titusville sent a man with a backhoe into a bog five miles from my parents' accident site to carve a road for a new subdivision. The backhoe operator arrived in the early mist, finished the last of his truck stop coffee, hoisted himself into his machinery's cab and switched on the ignition. Leaning on the controls, he dipped the great steel bucket into the swamp, ladling up a serving of underground, pivoting the bucket and boom to one side, emptying his catch on a mass of wild mustard. Sweating now, holding to the joystick, he heard an odd sound in the emptying: the chunk and clangor of a large rock, not the usual sigh and sizzle of mud and sand, so he switched off the power and eased himself out to take a look. What he found in the sliding earth, surfacing, rocking a little like a clam shell, was the curved top of a skull, a human one, and as the dirt fell away, he saw the skull was whole, intact, eye sockets rolling up toward the sky for the first time in a long time. Up, up, and up, as if they still held living, jellied eyes, brown pupils searching, to capture the sun and moon and stars, tuck them into the dark purse of the imagination.

For the first time in seven thousand years, that head, exposed. Naked, a bone globe, lolling in a lap of gumbo, the way a long-ago child napped against its mother's belly. Before anyone else came here. Before the written word.

The backhoe operator called the developer, and the developer called the county medical examiner, who said the skull was older than any unsolved murder in Brevard County. The developer called the anthropology department at Florida State, and a team of researchers swept down, drawing, with great care, white knots and candles of bone from the spoil banks. They estimated the bones at five hundred to six hundred years old, Florida soil and water being too acidic for longer preservation. Yet, to their wonderment, radiocarbon dating whisked the precious limbs back to prehistory, practically to myth.

For more than three years, the university team labored to uncover and examine the remains of the ancient individuals who had slept so long in the swamp. Wuesthoff Hospital, where my parents had been taken, and died, opened its expanded facilities for researchers to clean and categorize their finds. The most extraordinary artifact was a human brain, complete, safe in its skull. Other skulls held brain tissue, too—enough to share with laboratories over the world—and so the bits were dispersed to Denmark, Switzerland, Australia. A miracle, that remnants of what generated minds and souls so long ago could inform and enlighten the present.

By the time the archaeologists decided to stop, they had recovered 168 corpses or remains, leaving as many more to be met in the future, or simply to lie folded in repose. They called the revealed tribe Windover Bog People, for the new housing development, Windover Farms, which had never been a farm.

That a place refers to its developer, or its developer's dream, is a long tradition, of course. For my lifetime, I think of that postwar classic, Levittown, New York, named for its founder, William Levitt, or Plantation, a community between the beach and the Everglades my father helped sell in the early 1960s. The discovered's natural landscape (grassland for Levittown, marshland for Plantation), or the accurate descriptor given by earlier inhabitants (Hempstead Plains, Pine Island Ridge), is paved over, dressed up, even as the land is clawed and squared for house foundations and replanted with trucked-in greenery. Yet I don't care that Windover Farms never yielded one strawberry, one celery stalk. I'm taken instead by the miracle that, for seven thousand years, Florida's breezes tickled a nameless muck pond in Titusville and never lifted so much as a tooth from the quiet tomb, submerged, shrouded by the swinging shadows of live oak and slash pine. For seven thousand years, the Windover people, predecessors of the tribe Spanish explorers encountered in the sixteenth century, lay safe at home, steps away from their vanished shelters, from where they had first drawn breath. Everything they needed to live and thrive, said the scientists, had been close at hand.

In the three seasons Florida State's archaeologists spent at Windover, they uncovered hundreds of artifacts, pointing to the

kinds of lives the Bog People led. There were hammers, fash-
ioned from manatee ribs and wielded with wooden handles, still
functional; one hammer sported a dog tooth for extra punch. A
deer antler had been turned into an atlatl hook, the hook being
the end of the ancient launching device that sent spears clear
across a squishy marsh or hardwood hammock straight into the
flesh of the hunter's prey, which might be, of course, another
deer. A hollow bird bone, incised with pin thin lines, had probably served as a whistle—to call children, begin a hunt, sig-
nal distress, even, to play a primitive sort of song? Music pre-
ceded speech, so the theory goes, and it makes sense to me, that
after pure, open sound issued from our lungs and throats and
mouths—infant's cry, woman's groan, man's whoop—we varied
pitch to communicate, to express, to make melody, and finally,
with our lips, tongue, teeth, and throat, to articulate particular
speech, moving, over centuries, from gut body resonances to the
more cerebral equivalent of triple counterpoint. We were and are
simply manipulating streams of air, the source of life, of inspiration, breathing our way across time, shaping the breath as we
shape our lives, the two often converging in story.

It's likely that the hammers, the atlatl hook, and the whistle
were wielded by men, but I prefer to imagine the bog's whistle
virtuoso was a woman. I see her, a deeply tanned mother, about
five feet tall, her lean form wrapped lightly in a length of cloth
she has woven from fibers of palmetto and queen palm. She is
crouching over a heap of fresh snails harvested from the Saint
Johns River, rinsing them with water poured from a gourd, as
her children dart among the bushes, laughing, searching for
prickly pear to eat, a turtle to tease.

And now she notices the fizz and glide of a snake close by,
suspects it might be dangerous, that a child might encounter
it. She lifts the bird bone whistle to her lips, pushes her breath

high through the opening to sound a warning, the way birds do. The note is shrill, edgy. She repeats it twice, three times, and as the children pop out like lightning bugs among the scrub palmetto, she motions them behind her with her free arm. When the snake has passed, she exhales into the whistle leisurely, producing a softer, lower tone, indicating a catastrophe has been averted. All is well. Loud, soft. Tension, release. The will and tranquility of music, with which she experiments later that evening. Inhaling deeply, her center buoyant with air, she once again sends a firm gust into the whistle, but this time builds a more elegant gesture, a controlled arc upward, touching the roof of her range, hovering at the top of its curve, then, in the same long line, allows the sonority to dissipate, the pitch to fall. She has built a phrase, and can embellish it as she likes, breaking it here and there, lingering on one note and then another, like the bird she imitates, whose wing she plays.

Acknowledgments

For prompting this book: Richard C. "Dick" Bartlett (1935–2011).

For nurturing, editing, and publishing it: Shannon Davies, director, Texas A&M University Press; Jimmie Killingsworth, general editor, the Seventh Generation series; Katie Duelm, managing and project editor; Dawn Hall, copyeditor.

For generous support: The Thinking Like a Mountain Foundation, the University of North Texas.

For insightful research assistance: J. D. Smith, Anna Balka.

For quiet places to write: The Thinking Like a Mountain Foundation; Madroño Ranch: A Center for Writing, Art, and the Environment; the Byrdcliffe Colony; Kathy Allen-Weber and Alan Weber; Ellis Anderson and Larry Jaubert; Estalene McCutchan and Dennis Myers; Sandy Ostrom McInvale; Carolyn and Joe Osborn, Peter Parolin.

For great advice: Steve Hughes.

For great ideas: Pat Alexander, Jana Harris, Earl Robicheaux.

For splendid suggestions: Emily Fox Gordon, Mary Gilliland, Carolyn Osborn, Pat Alexander, Bonnie Friedman, Barbara Rodman, John Tait, Amos Magliocco.

For helpful resources: The Department of Special and Area Studies and Collections, George A. Smathers Library, University of Florida; North Brevard Historical Society; Suzan Shaw, Florida Department of Education; Canaveral National Seashore; Merritt Island National Wildlife Refuge; Dr. Glen Doran, Department of Anthropology, Florida State University; Bowdoin College Library, Bowdoin, Maine; Deanna Engler, University Archives and Special Collections, David L. Rice Library,

University of Southern Indiana; Keith Kutzler, registrar, University of Evansville; Vanderburgh County Clerk, Evansville, Indiana; Will McCutchan and William M. McCutchan (1954–2013); the Library of Congress.

For personal material: Estalene McCutchan, Beth Bond Dunn, Lynda Bond Pound, Patricia McCutchan Bass, and Bertie Gillespie; Brad Baker, Anne Foglia, Adrianne Foglia, and Alice F. Lucia; James Ansell, Stephanie Bardwell, Denise Blanchard-Boehm, Bruce Brown, Karen Keel Burroughs, Jay Carothers, Molly Carter Calhoun, Virginia Campbell, Debbie Clifton, Karen Smith Colclasure, Mike Dent, George Dunn, Jan Ewen Grimard, Patty Hepburn, Lin Herz, Tim Huffstickler, Greg High, Tom Hill, Jo Lynn Johnson Jorczak, John Kadlec, Bob Kemp, Mark Kimmel, Connie Lowe, Angela Lynch, Pat West Marovich, Joan Hare Massey, Sandy Ostrom McInvale, Sue Rex Michael, Wendy Dooley Morlan, Gary Rhinehart, Billy M. Rhodes, Barbara Hepburn Ross, Gerald Wayne Stephenson, Margaret Miller Vessels, and Cathy Sharpe Wilson.

For wanting to know how it all turned out: Leslie Brown Neal (1951–2014).

For wise teaching, in music, in life: Leon Russianoff (1916–1990).

Index